LIGHTHOUSES
OF THE ATLANTIC SEABOARD
A BOOK OF 21 POSTCARDS

W9-BVL-149

BROWNTROUT PUBLISHERS
SAN FRANCISCO • CALIFORNIA

BROWNTROUT PUBLISHERS
P.O. BOX 280070
SAN FRANCISCO • CALIFORNIA 94128-0070

ISBN: 1-56313-813-1
TITLE #: P6813

BROWNTROUT publishes a large line of calendars, photographic books, and postcard books.
Please write for more information.

Printed in Hong Kong

LIGHTHOUSES *of the* ATLANTIC SEABOARD
Nubble Lighthouse, Cape Neddick, Maine

BROWNTROUT PUBLISHERS • SAN FRANCISCO, CALIFORNIA

LIGHTHOUSES *of the* ATLANTIC SEABOARD
Rockland Breakwater Lighthouse, Rockland, Maine

BROWNTROUT PUBLISHERS • SAN FRANCISCO, CALIFORNIA

LIGHTHOUSES *of the* ATLANTIC SEABOARD
Cape Poge Lighthouse, Chappaquiddick Island, Massachusetts

BROWNTROUT PUBLISHERS • SAN FRANCISCO, CALIFORNIA

LIGHTHOUSES *of the* ATLANTIC SEABOARD
Barnegat Lighthouse, Island Beach State Park, New Jersey

BROWNTROUT PUBLISHERS • SAN FRANCISCO, CALIFORNIA

LIGHTHOUSES *of the* ATLANTIC SEABOARD
Long Point Lighthouse, Provincetown, Massachusetts

BROWNTROUT PUBLISHERS • SAN FRANCISCO, CALIFORNIA

LIGHTHOUSES *of the* ATLANTIC SEABOARD
Portland Head Lighthouse, Maine

BROWNTROUT PUBLISHERS • SAN FRANCISCO, CALIFORNIA

LIGHTHOUSES *of the* ATLANTIC SEABOARD
Cape Cod Lighthouse, Truro, Massachusetts

BROWNTROUT PUBLISHERS • SAN FRANCISCO, CALIFORNIA

BROWNTROUT PUBLISHERS · SAN FRANCISCO, CALIFORNIA

LIGHTHOUSES *of the* ATLANTIC SEABOARD
Watch Hill Lighthouse, Rhode Island

BROWNTROUT PUBLISHERS • SAN FRANCISCO, CALIFORNIA

LIGHTHOUSES *of the* ATLANTIC SEABOARD
Nauset Lighthouse, Eastham, Massachusetts

BROWNTROUT PUBLISHERS • SAN FRANCISCO, CALIFORNIA

LIGHTHOUSES *of the* ATLANTIC SEABOARD
Owl's Head Lighthouse, Maine

BROWNTROUT PUBLISHERS • SAN FRANCISCO, CALIFORNIA

LIGHTHOUSES *of the* ATLANTIC SEABOARD
Quoddy Head Lighthouse, Lubec, Maine

BROWNTROUT PUBLISHERS • SAN FRANCISCO, CALIFORNIA

LIGHTHOUSES *of the* ATLANTIC SEABOARD
Cape May Lighthouse, New Jersey

BROWNTROUT PUBLISHERS • SAN FRANCISCO, CALIFORNIA

LIGHTHOUSES *of the* ATLANTIC SEABOARD
Wood End Lighthouse, Cape Cod National Seashore,
Massachusetts

BROWNTROUT PUBLISHERS • SAN FRANCISCO, CALIFORNIA

LIGHTHOUSES *of the* ATLANTIC SEABOARD
Bass Head Lighthouse, Mt. Desert Island, Maine

BROWNTROUT PUBLISHERS • SAN FRANCISCO, CALIFORNIA

LIGHTHOUSES *of the* ATLANTIC SEABOARD
Pemaquid Point Lighthouse, Maine

BROWNTROUT PUBLISHERS • SAN FRANCISCO, CALIFORNIA

LIGHTHOUSES *of the* ATLANTIC SEABOARD
Gay Head Lighthouse, Martha's Vineyard, Massachusetts

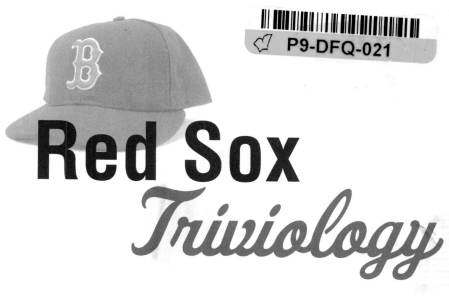

Red Sox
Triviology

Fascinating Facts from the Bleacher Seats

Christopher Walsh

TRIUMPH
B O O K S

Library of Congress Cataloging-in-Publication Data

Names: Walsh, Christopher J., 1968- author.
Title: Red sox triviology : fascinating facts from the bleacher seats / Christopher Walsh.
Description: Chicago, Illinois : Triumph Books, 2016.
Identifiers: LCCN 2016001677 | ISBN 9781629372372 (paperback)
Subjects: LCSH: Boston Red Sox (Baseball team)—History. | Boston Red Sox (Baseball team)—Miscellanea. | BISAC: TRAVEL / United States / Northeast / New England (CT, MA, ME, NH, RI, VT). | SPORTS & RECREATION / Baseball /
  History. | GAMES / Trivia.
Classification: LCC GV875.B62 W33 2016 | DDC 796.357/6409744—dc23 LC record available at http://lccn.loc.gov/2016001677

This book is available in quantity at special discounts for your group or organization. For further information, contact:

Triumph Books LLC
814 North Franklin Street
Chicago, Illinois 60610
(312) 676-4247
www.triumphbooks.com

Printed in U.S.A.
ISBN: 978-1-62937-237-2
Design by Meghan Grammer
All photos are courtesy of AP Images.

SPECIAL THANKS
To Noah Amstadter, Tom Bast, Jesse Jordan and everyone else at Triumph Books who worked on this project.

To the Red Sox Nation, but especially those
from the University of New Hampshire

"All I want out of life is when I walk down the street people say, 'There goes the greatest hitter that ever lived.'"
—*Ted Williams*

Contents

Introduction

It was the fall of 1986 and I was a freshman the University of New Hampshire. I had grown up a sports nut and for years my birthday was celebrated with a trip to Met Stadium to see the Minnesota Twins face the Boston Red Sox or New York Yankees, but nothing had quite prepared me for my first couple of months on campus when the New York Mets and the Red Sox were on a collision course to meet in the World Series.

The whole region went nuts. I mean really, really nuts, which was fitting considering the way things played out on the diamond, yet that was my first taste of what people meant when they said that Boston and New York were baseball cities. With each big victory along the way impromptu celebrations broke out and lasted well into the morning hours.

Two friends down the hall had a TV and we'd all cram into their room to watch every game, with those rooting for the Red Sox on one side and the Mets fans on the other (being the "foreigner" from Minnesota, I sat in the middle). When the ball went between Bill Buckner's legs in Game 6 everyone screamed, some in joy, others in absolute horror. My roommate, who had been making celebration plans, froze and sat in shock staring at the TV for about 90 minutes after we turned both it and the lights off.

Thankfully, the Red Sox came back and eventually won the World Series in 2004, and New England has had more than its fair share of championships in other sports as well. But I never looked at October and November baseball the same way again.

Hopefully some of that will come through in the pages to follow.

In putting this book together my aim wasn't to be overly easy or difficult, or have it serve as a quiz to measure the baseball IQ of even the most die-hard fans, but rather to celebrate, honor and inform. The Red Sox are one of the most interesting and colorful franchises to have ever existed, and it's hard to believe sometimes that they've been around for more than 100 years.

The book is organized into sections, and sometimes subsections, to make it easy to use. The questions range in difficulty from "No, duh" to extremely difficult, and those in the Hot Box section are practically impossible.

Above all else, I hope you enjoy it and learn a few things along the way.

One

The Basics

To really understand the origins of the Red Sox, one really has to go back to the late 1800s, when Boston was really at the center of the baseball world.

At the time the idea of professional baseball was in its infancy and the National Association of Professional Base Ball Players was anything but stable. Created in 1871, its franchises were unstable and many were located in cities that were too small to support such a venture.

There was also a lack of central authority and one team in particular, the Boston Red Stockings, who won the championship every year between 1872–75, dominated the league.

In part because five of his star players were on the verge of being kicked out of the NAPBBP, Chicago businessman William Hulbert started rallying support for the creation of a new league. It took him several years to convince enough owners to make the switch, but finally in 1876 the National League was born. The American League would join it in 1901.

The Red Stockings were mostly known as the Red Caps their first few years and then as the Beaneaters. Now they're known as the Atlanta Braves.

The Basics

1.   What was the team's nickname in 1901?
2.   Name two of its other nicknames during its initial years.
3.   When was the team first called the Red Sox?
4.   Who came up with the Red Sox nickname and when was it first used?
5.   What move by another team precipitated the change?
6.   Why did that team make such a change?
7.   What is that team known as now?
8.   Where did the team play home games before Fenway Park?
9.   What other team did Charles W. Somers also own?
10.   Who did Boston face in its first official game?
11.   What well-known pitcher got the franchise's first win?
12.   In what place in the standings did Boston finish during its first season?
13.   True or false, in 1906 Boston was the first American League team to lose 100 games.
14.   Through 2015 how many World Series has the franchise won?
15.   How many times has it played in the World Series?
16.   In what year did the Red Sox win the American League title but not play in the World Series?
17.   How many times have the Red Sox hosted an All-Star Game?
18.   Who are the four Red Sox named MVP of the All-Star Game?
19.   What's the name of the team mascot?
20.   What Red Sox owner is in the National Baseball Hall of Fame?

The 1999 All-Star Game at Fenway will always be remembered for the pre-game appearance of Ted Williams, who players gathered around to meet. Here, Tony Gwynn helps Williams throw the ceremonial first pitch. (Matt York)

Answers

1. Americans
2. Somersets (after owner Charles W. Somers), Plymouth Rocks, Speed Boys, Puritans or Pilgrims.
3. 1907 (December 18th to be specific).
4. Owner John I. Taylor before the 1908 season.
5. At the time most baseball teams were identified by a color. When the crosstown Boston Red Stockings changed their name to "Doves" and switched from red to blue, the franchise quickly claimed the color and changed its nickname to "Red Sox."
6. Manager Fred Tenney believed that the red dye in the socks could possibly cause infection in spike wounds.
7. The Atlanta Braves
8. Huntington Avenue Grounds, which is now part of the Northeastern University campus.
9. The Cleveland Indians
10. The Baltimore Orioles, who won 10–6.
11. Cy Young
12. Second, behind the Chicago White Stockings.
13. False. Boston lost 100 games, but the Washington Senators lost 113 in 1904.
14. Eight
15. 12
16. 1904
17. Three: 1946, 1961 and 1999
18. 1970 Carl Yastrzemski; 1986 Roger Clemens; 1999 Pedro Martinez; 2008 J.D. Drew
19. Wally the Green Monster
20. Tom Yawkey

Two

Major League History

To put into perspective how long Major League Baseball has been around, consider what was going on when both leagues were created.

The National League was formed in 1876. That's the year Colorado became the 38th state, General George Armstrong Custer was killed along with 264 of his Union Calvary after engaging the Sioux tribe at Little Big Horn, and Thomas Edison had yet to invent the light bulb.

The American league came around in 1901. That's before the Wright Brothers made their first flight (1903), the San Francisco Earthquake (1906) and Ford introduced the Model-T car (1908). The president at the time was William McKinley, who was beginning his second term when he was shot and fatally wounded by an anarchist on the grounds of the Pan-American Exposition in Buffalo, New York, on September 6.

Theodore Roosevelt was promptly sworn in as his successor. Although he wasn't a big fan of the game, in 1907 the National Association of Professional Baseball Leagues issued him the first presidential lifetime pass, which was made of 14-karat gold.

Major League History

1. What was the original name of the National League?
2. Name the original eight teams.
3. Which two still exist?
4. Which two organizations were kicked out of the league during the first year, and why?
5. What happened to the other four teams that are no longer in existence?
6. Which two teams that are still in the National League joined in 1883?
7. Where was the first National League game played?
8. Who had the first hit in National League history?
9. Who is credited with scoring the first run?
10. Who had the first home run?
11. Who threw the first no-hitter?
12. What major innovation occurred in 1877?
13. Although many upstart leagues would challenge the National League, which was its first significant rival?
14. Which four teams switched allegiances and joined the National League prior to 1892?
15. When the two leagues essentially merged, which four franchises joined the National League in 1892?
16. Which one of those four continues to exist today?
17. Before it developed into a Major League what was the American League known as?
18. When the American League was formally organized in 1901 it had eight teams. Name them (nicknames included).
19. Which three original American Association clubs were dropped when the American League formed?
20. What future nemesis of the Red Sox was awarded a franchise in 1903 when the original Baltimore Orioles failed?

Answers

1. The National League of Professional Baseball
2. The Boston Red Stockings, Chicago White Stockings, Cincinnati Red Legs, Hartford Dark Blues, Louisville Grays, Philadelphia Athletics, Brooklyn Mutuals and St. Louis Browns
3. The Boston Red Stockings are now the Atlanta Braves. The Chicago Cubs are the only original team that never moved.
4. After falling behind in the standings the Athletics and Mutuals refused to make western road trips late in the season, opting to instead play local teams to save money. Hulbert expelled them.
5. Three of them folded within two years. The Cincinnati Red Stockings were expelled after the 1880 season.
6. The New York Gothams and Philadelphia Phillies. The Gothams are now known as the San Francisco Giants.
7. Philadelphia's Jefferson Street Grounds, 25th & Jefferson. Boston defeated the hometown team 6–5.
8. Jim O'Rourke
9. Tim McGinley
10. Chicago's Ross Barnes. Cincinnati's William "Cherokee" Fisher was the pitcher.
11. St. Louis' George Bradley, against Hartford.
12. Al Spalding made the first major league baseball glove
13. The American Association (1882–91), which eventually disbanded.
14. The teams now known as the Cincinnati Reds, Los Angeles Dodgers, Pittsburgh Pirates and the now-defunct Cleveland Spiders.
15. The Baltimore Orioles, Louisville Colonels, St. Louis Perfectos and the Washington Senators.
16. The St. Louis Perfectos, who became the St. Louis Cardinals. The other three were contracted after the 1899 season. The team now called the Baltimore Orioles was the St. Louis Browns, who moved in 1953.
17. The Western League.
18. The American League formally organized with the Baltimore Orioles, Philadelphia Athletics, Boston Somersets, Washington Nationals, Cleveland Blues, Detroit Tigers, Milwaukee Brewers, and Chicago White Stockings.
19. The clubs from Indianapolis, Minneapolis, and Buffalo were dropped.
20. The New York Highlanders, who were called so by the media due to playing at Hilltop Park, along with "Yanks."

Three

Famous Firsts

One of the reasons why the 86-year World Series drought was so painful for Boston baseball fans was that the franchise had one of the first dynasties in the sport.

From 1912 to 1918 it won four World Series and also had two 100-win seasons before the 162-game schedule. It also played in a modern stadium and had some of the premier players in the game.

It also won the first World Series ever played, but more about that later...

Babe Ruth played for the 1916 and '18 Red Sox World Series squads, pitching to a combined 3–0 record with a 0.87 ERA.

Famous Firsts

1. Where did Boston play its first game, which team won and what was the score?
2. Against which opponent did Boston notch the franchise's first victory?
3. At the end of its first week of play, and the day after it lost 14–1, Boston set the league's season high for runs scored in a game. What was it?
4. Who led Boston in hitting during its first season?
5. Who was the first player to hit both an inside-the-park home run and a conventional home run in the same game?
6. Who was the first player in franchise history to hit for the cycle?
7. Who was the first Red Sox pitcher to throw a shutout in his Major League debut?
8. When Cy Young threw the first perfect game in Major League history in 1904, which former Red Sox was catching for the other team and would become the only catcher in history to be on the losing side of two perfect games?
9. Which team won the game the first time the franchise used the Red Sox nickname?
10. After losing a no-hitter in the ninth inning of his previous start, who threw one in 1911?
11. The first times a Red Sox player won a Gold Glove and Silver Slugger award both were by a third baseman. Name them.
12. What sort of "first" did Red Sox first baseman Stuffy McInnis do on June 23, 1922?
13. Who was the first player in Major League history to hit 50-plus home runs during a single season with two different teams?
14. Who was the first general manger in franchise history?
15. Who was the first Red Sox to hit a home run in his first plate appearance for the team?

16. True or false, Ted Williams hit his first Major League home run, his first multiple home-run game and first grand slam all during the same season.
17. True or false, the first player in Major League history to hit two grand slams in one game was a Red Sox.
18. Who was the first Red Sox to not only hit a cycle twice, but also do them a decade apart?
19. Who was the first Red Sox to hit an inside-the-park home run in his first plate appearance for the team?
20. Who was the first player to win the American League Rookie of the Year award by a unanimous vote?
21. Who hit home runs in both of the first two games he played in the majors?
22. Who was the first Red Sox rookie to throw a no-hitter?
23. Who hit the first pitch he saw in the major leagues for a home run?
24. What Red Sox pitcher won his first 14 decisions against the Baltimore Orioles?
25. Who is listed first on the franchise's all-time roster?

Answers

1. The Baltimore Orioles, who won 10–6 at Oriole Park on April 26, 1901.
2. The Philadelphia Athletics, 8–6
3. It crushed the Philadelphia Athletics 23–12.
4. Jimmy Collins had 187 hits and an average of .332
5. Buck Freeman vs. Cleveland on July 17, 1901.
6. Buck Freeman against the Cleveland Naps on June 21, 1903
7. Rube Kroh 2–0 at St. Louis on September 30, 1906. He gave up just two hits.
8. Ossee Schreckengost
9. Boston defeated the Washington Senators, 3–1, on April 14, 1908.
10. Smoky Joe Wood
11. Frank Malzone won the franchise's first Gold Glove in 1957, and Carney Lansford won a Silver Slugger in 1981.
12. He made his first fielding error in over a year.
13. Jimmie Foxx in 1938 when he hit 50 home runs with the Boston Red Sox. He hit 58 with the Philadelphia Athletics in 1932.
14. Eddie Collins (1933–47).
15. Lefty LeFebvre vs. the Chicago White Sox on June 10, 1938. It was also his first at-bat in the Major Leagues.
16. True, all in 1939. His first home run was April 21, when he went 4-for-5 in a 12–8 loss to the Philadelphia Athletics at Fenway Park. He hit two home runs in a game for the first time on May 4, and he hit the grand slam on August 19.
17. False. It was Tony Lazzeri of the New York Yankees on May 24, 1936.
18. Joe Cronin. He did the first in 1929 and the second in 1940. He also did the second one as a player/manager, inserting himself into the lineup and helping lead a 12–9 victory against the Detroit Tigers.
19. John Kennedy against Cleveland on July 5, 1970.
20. Carlton Fisk in 1972.
21. Sam Horn on July 25–26, 1987.
22. Clay Buchholz as Boston beat the Baltimore Orioles 10–0 on September 1, 2007.
23. Daniel Nava on June 12, 2010 vs. the Philadelphia Phillies.
24. Jon Lester, from August 13, 2006 to April 28, 2011.
25. Pitcher David Aardsma (2008–09)

Four

Fenway Park

The Boston Red Sox are pretty much unique in that they've been around for more than 100 years, yet have only had two homes—and most people don't care much about the first one.

Built in 1912, world-renowned Fenway Park is the oldest facility in American professional sports, and on the National Register of Historic Places.

Because it was built in the dense Fenway–Kenmore neighborhood, which led to some unusual space limitations, it features the most unique left-field wall in baseball and some unusual ground rules:

- Foul poles are inside the field of play.
- A ball going through the scoreboard, either on the bounce or fly, is a ground rule double.
- A fly ball striking left-center field wall to right of or on the line behind the flagpole is a home run.
- A fly ball striking wall or flagpole and bouncing into bleachers is a home run.
- A fly ball striking line or right of same on wall in center is a home run.
- A fly ball striking wall left of line and bouncing into bullpen is a home run.
- A ball sticking in the bullpen screen or bouncing into the bullpen is a ground rule double.

- A batted or thrown ball remaining behind or under canvas or in tarp cylinder is a ground-rule double.
- A ball striking the top of the scoreboard in left field in the ladder below top of wall and bouncing out of the park is a ground-rule double.
- A fly ball that lands above the red line on top of the Green Monster and bounces onto the field of play is ruled a home run.
- A fly ball that hits the rail in the right-center triangle (region of the outfield) is a home run.

Despite numerous renovations and upgrades Fenway Park has maintained both an intimacy that other stadiums are now trying to duplicate, and charm that makes it a must-visit for baseball fans everywhere.

Fenway Park

1. What's the address for Fenway Park?
2. What was the original address?
3. What did it cost to build?
4. Who was the owner of the Red Sox at the time?
5. On April 9, 1912, what non-Major League team did the Red Sox face in an exhibition game at Fenway Park?
6. Who did the Red Sox face in the first official game at Fenway Park on April 20, 1912?
7. Who knocked in the winning run in the 11th inning?
8. What overshadowed the opening in terms of media coverage?
9. Who hit the first home run at Fenway Park?
10. Who threw the first no-hitter at Fenway Park?
11. The first college football game at Fenway Park was played between which two schools on October 31, 1914?
12. What part of Fenway Park burned down on May 8, 1926?

13. How many alarms was the second Fenway Park fire in 1934?
14. Why did the Red Sox play their Sunday games at Braves Field on Commonwealth Avenue from 1929–32?
15. Who gave the final speech of his political career before 40,000 supporters at Fenway Park?
16. On June 9, 1946, Ted Williams hit an estimated 502-foot home run against Detroit at Fenway Park. Where did it land?
17. What marks that spot now?
18. Who went 4-for-4 with two home runs, five RBIs and four runs scored during the 1946 All-Star Game at Fenway Park?
19. Which team won the first basketball game played at Fenway Park in 1954?
20. Where is "Williamsburg?"
21. How tall is the left-field wall known as the "Green Monster?"
22. How long is the Green Monster?
23. How far is it from home plate?
24. Before the Green Monster was green, what was on it?
25. On the 100th anniversary of Fenway Park, who debuted his gift to the club and stadium, "Fanfare for Fenway?"
26. What was renamed in his honor on September 27, 2006, on Johnny Pesky's 87th birthday?
27. As of 2015 there are three statues that stand outside of Fenway Park. Who are they of?
28. True or false, a fly ball that gets stuck in the ladder above the scoreboard on the left-field wall is ruled a ground-rule triple.
29. What attendance streak came to an end in April 2013?
30. What song is traditionally played over the ballpark's speakers before the bottom of the 8th inning?
31. Who sang it during the 8th inning of the Red Sox-Kansas City Royals game in Fenway Park on April 20, 2013, a few days after the Boston Marathon bombing?

Answers

1. 4 Yawkey Way near Kenmore Square
2. 24 Jersey Street
3. $350,000
4. John I. Taylor
5. Harvard
6. The New York Highlanders
7. Tris Speaker
8. The sinking of the Titanic a few days earlier.
9. First baseman Hugh Bradley on April 26, 1912. It was the second, and last, home run of his career.
10. George Davis of the Boston Braves, to lead a 7–0 victory over Philadelphia on Sept. 9, 1914.
11. Boston College and Norwich University. BC won 28–6.
12. The bleacher seats along the left-field foul line.
13. Five. The fire destroyed a lot of the construction underway by new owner Tom Yawkey.
14. Because Fenway Park was close to a church.
15. Franklin D. Roosevelt on Nov. 4, 1944
16. According to the Red Sox Media Guide the ball landed on top of the straw hat of Joseph A. Boucher, a 56-year-old construction engineer from Albany, N.Y., who was sitting in Section 42, Row 37, Seat 21. "The sun was right in our eyes," he said. "All we could do was duck. I'm glad I didn't stand up. They say it bounced a dozen rows higher, but after it hit my head, I was no longer interested."
17. The lone red seat in the right-field bleachers. All the other seats are green.
18. Ted Williams. The American League won 12–0.
19. The Harlem Globetrotters
20. It's the bullpen area built in front of the right-center field bleachers in 1940, primarily so left-handed batters like Ted Williams would be 23 feet closer to hitting home runs.
21. 37 feet high.
22. 231 feet (228 in fair territory).
23. 310 feet from home plate.
24. Ads
25. John Williams, who conducted the Boston Pops during the celebration.
26. The right-field foul pole. "Pesky's Pole" is only 302 feet from home plate.
27. "The Kid" is of Ted Williams with a Jimmy Fund Kid. "Teammates" depicts Williams, Bobby Doerr, Johnny Pesky, and Dom DiMaggio. Carl Yastrzemski's statue is of him acknowledging the fans before his last at-bat with the Red Sox in 1983. It was dedicated in 2013.
28. False. It's a myth among Red Sox fans. There is no such thing in the Major Leagues, but there is a three-base award if a player attempts to use his hat to alter the path of a ball, either in the air or on the ground in fair territory.
29. The Red Sox' regular-season sellout streak of 794 consecutive regular season games, which dated back to May 15, 2003 and was the longest recorded regular-season sellout streak in United States professional sports history.
30. Sweet Caroline
31. Neil Diamond

Five

Nicknames

What's in a nickname? A lot, especially when it comes to naming a sports organization.

Boston has been home to some epic and unique franchises, and not just in baseball. Basketball has the Celtics, football the Patriots and the Bruins were one of the Original Six franchises in the National Hockey League.

But Boston is still a baseball town, and when you say Red Sox anywhere in the United States there's no doubt about what team is being discussed, although one will hear numerous slang variations of the name:

- The Sox
- The Sawx is Sox spoken with a Boston accent (and often badly imitated).
- The BoSox is a combination of Boston and Sox.
- The Crimson Hose
- The Olde Towne Team
- Red Sox Nation is a reference to avid followers of the team, who extend well beyond Boston.
- The Nation is a short version of "Red Sox Nation".
- The Cardiac Kids, a nickname for the 1967 team.

Nicknames

As for the players, who had the following nicknames?

1. Mr. Red Sox
2. Old Folks
3. Sal the Barber
4. Double X
5. Laser Show
6. Rocket
7. Yaz
8. Big Papi
9. The Terminator
10. The Kid
11. Spaceman
12. Dice K
13. The Gerbil
14. The Little Professor
15. Dr. Strangeglove
16. The Dirt Dog
17. Grey Eagle
18. Pudge
19. Mr. Clutch and "Dutch the Clutch."
20. Tomato
21. Tony C
22. D-Lew
23. Eck
24. The Greek God of Walks
25. Tek
26. Dewey
27. The Hit Dog
28. El Guapo
29. Oil Can
30. Jim Ed

Can you remember Mo Vaughn's nickname?

Answers

1. Johnny Pesky
2. Ellis Kinder
3. Sal Maglie
4. Jimmie Foxx, also known as "The Beast"
5. Dustin Pedroia, also known as "La Luna"
6. Roger Clemens
7. Carl Yastrzemski
8. David Ortiz. He's also known as "Señor Octubre"
9. Jeff Reardon
10. Ted Williams
11. Bill Lee
12. Daisuke Matsuzaka
13. Don Zimmer
14. Dom DiMaggio
15. Dick Stuart
16. Trot Nixon
17. Tris Speaker
18. Carlton Fisk
19. Joe Cronin and Clyde Vollmer.
20. Jack Lamabe
21. Tony Conigliaro
22. Darren Lewis
23. Dennis Eckersley
24. Kevin Youkilis
25. Jason Varitek
26. Dwight Evans
27. Mo Vaughn
28. Rich Garces
29. Dennis Boyd
30. Jim Rice

Six

The Greats

For most baseball fans there really is only one true Boston Red Sox, Ted Williams.

He was so good that Williams had numerous nicknames, including "The Kid," "The Splendid Splinter," "Teddy Ballgame," "The Thumper," and "The Greatest Hitter Who Ever Lived."

"Baseball is the only field of endeavor where a man can succeed three times out of ten and be considered a good performer," he once said, but no one may have been better at it than he.

Despite serving in the military during two wars during the prime of his career, Williams was a six-time batting champion and also led the American League in home runs and RBIs four times each.

The last man to hit .400 in a season, his career on-base percentage is considered one of those records that may be unbreakable.

Since Williams retired, only four players have posted an OBP above .482 in a season, with Barry Bonds the only one to do so more than once. Bonds ended his career with an OBP of .444, and the next-closest player to Williams in career OBP is Babe Ruth at .474.

"Did they tell me how to pitch to Williams? Sure they did," Bobby Shantz, the 1952 American League MVP, said. "It was great advice, very encouraging. They said he had no weakness, won't swing at a bad ball, has the best eyes in the business, and can kill you with one swing. He won't hit anything bad, but don't give him anything good."

"One of my best friends on earth and the greatest hitter I ever faced. And I faced a lot of guys, including Lou Gehrig," Bob Feller surmised.

Although he may not have been the first Red Sox inducted into the National Baseball Hall of Fame, Williams has the honor of being listed here first (the rest are alphabetical):

Ted Williams

1. What two people are Ted Williams named after?
2. Where was he born on August 30, 1918?
3. Who were his baseball heroes while growing up?
4. Where did he attend high school?
5. Which two Major League teams offered him a contract while he was still in high school, and why did he turn them down?
6. In 1938, why was Williams 10 days late to his first spring training?
7. When he arrived who nicknamed him "The Kid"?
8. Which legendary player was on the opposing side when Williams made his Major League debut on April 20, 1939, and it was the only time they faced one another in a game?
9. The same pitcher who had given Williams his first strikeout as a professional baseball player in San Diego also yielded his first home run at Fenway Park. Who was he?
10. True or false, Williams was the first rookie to lead the American League in RBIs.
11. Why did Williams only play in 89 games during the 1950 season?
12. In 1956 who edged Williams for the American League batting title to win the triple crown (leading in batting average, home runs and RBIs)?
13. Williams is one of only four players to hit a home run in each of four different decades. Name the other three.

14. What father-son combination did Williams hit home runs off of?
15. Who is the only other player in Major League history to hit home runs off a father-son combination?
16. On April 30, 1952, what did Williams do at the plate in his final at-bat before going overseas in the Korean War as a Marine fighter pilot?
17. How many grand slams did Williams hit for the Red Sox, and how many home runs did he hit as a pinch-hitter?
18. In 1949, how many consecutive games did Williams get on base?
19. In what two years did Williams win the American League triple crown?
20. True or false, he also was named league MVP both of those years.
21. On August 24, 1940, Williams pitched two innings during a 12–1 loss to the Detroit Tigers. Who did he strike out and who was his catcher?
22. True or false, Williams was the manager for the last Washington Senators game in 1971, and the first Texas Rangers game in 1972 after the franchise moved.
23. How many hits did Williams have on the final day of the 1941 season to finish with a batting average above .400?
24. Williams famously hit a home run in his final at-bat, off the pitcher who gave up Roger Maris' 60th home run of the 1961 season (September 26, 1961), and the first home run in Shea Stadium history to Willie Stargell (April 17, 1964). Name him.
25. When Williams was elected into the National Baseball Hall of Fame in 1966 he received 93.4 percent of the vote in his first year of eligibility. Name the only four inductees who received a higher percentage of votes prior to 1966.

Answers

1. Teddy Samuel Williams was named after his father, Samuel Stuart Williams, and former president Teddy Roosevelt.
2. San Diego, California
3. Pepper Martin of the St. Louis Cardinals and Bill Terry of the New York Giants.
4. Herbert Hoover High School in San Diego.
5. The New York Yankees and St. Louis Cardinals, but because his mother thought he was too young to leave home he signed with the then minor-league San Diego Padres.
6. A flood in California kept the railroads from running.
7. Red Sox equipment manager Johnny Orlando.
8. Lou Gehrig
9. Cotton Pippen
10. True
11. During the first inning of the All-Star Game he slammed into the Comiskey Park scoreboard while catching a Ralph Kiner line drive and broke his left arm. He stayed in the game and knocked in a run, but later had surgery.
12. Mickey Mantle
13. Rickey Henderson, Willie McCovey and Omar Vizquel.
14. Thornton Lee on September 17, 1939, and his son Don Lee on September 2, 1960.
15. Andre Dawson: Pedro Borbon on June 10, 1977, and Pedro Borbon (Jr.) on August 16, 1995.
16. He hit a game-winning, two-run home run off Detroit's Dizzy Trout to lead a 5–3 victory.
17. 17 and seven
18. .84
19. 1942 (36 home runs, .356 average and 137 RBIs) and 1947 (32, .343, 114, respectively). He's the only player in American League history to do so twice.
20. False. Joe Gordon won in 1942 and Joe DiMaggio won in 1947.
21. Williams struck out Rudy York on three pitches, and his catcher was Joe Glenn, who caught for Babe Ruth's last pitching appearance in 1933.
22. True
23. Six during a doubleheader. The day before manager Joe Cronin offered to sit him and Williams refused, only to see his average drop from .401 to .3995 after going 1-for-4. Williams went 4-for-5 in the first game and 2-for-3 in the second game.
24. Jack Fisher.
25. Ty Cobb, Honus Wagner, Babe Ruth, and Bob Feller.

Wade Boggs

1. Where was Wade Boggs born on June 15, 1958?
2. Where was he a two-sport star in high school?
3. What position in another sport did he stop playing as a senior in high school to protect his baseball career?
4. What college still offered him a scholarship as a punter and kicker?
5. What round was he selected in the 1976 draft?
6. In 1981 Boggs participated in the longest game in professional baseball history, lasting 33 innings over eight hours and 25 minutes. Boggs finished the game with four hits in 12 at-bats, and drove in the tying run in the 21st inning for what winning team?
7. What future Hall of Fame player was on the losing side of that game?
8. How old was Boggs when he made his Major League debut?
9. What kept Boggs from winning the American League batting title as a rookie?
10. How many batting titles did Boggs win with the Red Sox?
11. True or false, Boggs once won both the Silver Slugger and Gold Glove award during the same season.
12. In 1987 Boggs hit a career-high number of home runs. His second most was 11 in 1994. How many did he hit in '87?
13. How many home runs did he hit the following season when he had a career high 125 RBIs?
14. Who broke his American League record of seven consecutive seasons with 200 hits?
15. Which team has retired Boggs' No. 12?
16. Why did Jim Rice once call Boggs "Chicken Man?"
17. How man ground balls would Boggs take in pre-game practice?
18. Why did he also take batting practice at 5:17 p.m. for night games and run sprints at 7:17?

Wade Boggs holds up the champagne bottle after a Game 7 victory over the California Angels sent the Red Sox to the 1986 World Series. (Peter Southwick)

19. What did he draw in the batter's box before every at-bat?
20. Why did Boggs ask Fenway Park announcer Sherm Feller to not say his uniform number when being introduced?

Answers

1. Omaha, Nebraska
2. Plant High School in Tampa, Florida.
3. Quarterback
4. South Carolina
5. Seventh
6. The Pawtucket Red Sox of the Triple-A International League.
7. Cal Ripken Jr. of the Rochester Red Wings.
8. 23
9. He had a .349 batting average, but was 121 plate appearances short of the required minimum of 502.
10. Five (1983, 1985–88)
11. True, 1994. He won two Gold Gloves (1994 and 1995), and eight Silver Sluggers (1983, 1986–1989, 1991, 1993, 1994).
12. 24
13. Five
14. Ichiro Suzuki
15. The Tampa Bay Rays, with whom he finished his career (1998–99).
16. Boggs ate chicken before every game. It was one of his many superstitions.
17. Exactly 117
18. In hopes of going 7-for-7 at the plate
19. Hebrew word "Chai," meaning "life" (despite not being Jewish).
20. Because Boggs once broke out of a slump on a day when Feller forgot to announce his number.

Roger Clemens

1. Where was Roger Clemens born on August 4, 1962?
2. Where did he begin his collegiate career?
3. With which school did he win the College World Series?
4. What NCAA record did Clemens hold until Justin Pope broke it in 2011?
5. The Roger Clemens Award honors the best pitcher in college baseball, but what award by the Greater Houston Sports Association did it replace in 2004?
6. With what pick did the Red Sox select Clemens in the first round of the 1983 draft?
7. In 1986, what did Clemens become the first starting pitcher to do since Vida Blue in 1971?
8. How many complete games did Clemens have in 1987 and why was it significant?
9. Who was Clemens talking about and why when he said: "I wish he were still playing. I'd probably crack his head open to show him how valuable I was."
10. On June 21, 1989, who hit his first career home run off Clemens?
11. What was Clemens' ERA during the 1990 season when he went 21–6?
12. True or false, Clemens had a losing record his last season with the Red Sox.
13. How many career wins did Clemens have?
14. How many career strikeouts did he notch?
15. Which number is the highest, times Clemens led the Major Leagues in wins, either league in ERA, or the American League in strikeouts?
16. What statistical accomplishment did Clemens do twice with the Toronto Blue Jays that he was never able to pull off with the Red Sox?
17. How many times did Clemens win the Cy Young Award?
18. Not only was Clemens the first pitcher in Major League history to strike out 20 batters in a nine-inning game, but he did it a second time 10 years later. Name the two opponents.

19. How old was Clemens when he won his last Cy Young Award, and what team was he playing for?
20. Clemens became the fourth pitcher in Major League history to win a Cy Young in both leagues. Who were the first three?

Answers

1. Dayton, Ohio
2. San Jacinto College North, located just outside of Houston.
3. Texas
4. He pitched 35 consecutive scoreless innings.
5. The Rotary Smith Award
6. 19th.
7. Win a league MVP award.
8. 18. No pitcher has matched that since.
9. Hank Aaron after the former slugger said pitchers should not be eligible for the MVP award.
10. Sammy Sosa, who was a rookie with the Texas Rangers.
11. 1.93
12. True, he was 10–13 for his second losing season in four years.
13. 354
14. 4,672
15. He was a league's ERA champion seven times, the American League strikeout king five times, and topped the majors in wins four times.
16. He won two pitching Triple Crowns (he led the league in wins, strikeouts and earned run average), which he did in 1987–88.
17. Seven (1986, 1987, 1991, 1997, 1998, 2001, 2004), the most of any pitcher in Major League history.
18. The Seattle Mariners on April 29, 1986, and the Detroit Tigers on September 18, 1996
19. 42, for the Houston Astros. He's the oldest pitcher to win the award.
20. Gaylord Perry, Pedro Martinez and Randy Johnson.

Jimmy Collins

1. Where was Jimmy Collins born on January 16, 1870?
2. Where did he attend prep school?
3. What was his primary source of income after graduating?
4. With which team did he begin his professional baseball career?
5. With which team did Collins first play for in what would become the major leagues?
6. How much did it cost that team to buy out his contract and acquire his services?
7. To which team was he loaned during the 1895 season?
8. What did his parent team get in exchange?
9. What was Collins especially known for defensively?
10. In what defensive category did he more often than not lead the league?
11. What offensive category did Collins lead the National League in 1898?
12. How were the upstart Boston Americans in the new American League able to lure him away?
13. What rare franchise first did Collins do as a player during the 1902 season?
14. Who replaced Collins as manager in 1906?
15. What happened to him before the start of the next season?
16. To which team was Collins traded during the 1907 season?
17. What did Boston get in return?
18. For the first time in his major league career, what did Collins fail to do during the 1907 season?
19. Name one of the two minor-league teams that Collins played for/managed before retiring from baseball.
20. What Hall of Fame first was Collins?

Answers

1. Buffalo, New York
2. St. Joseph's Collegiate Institute
3. He worked for the Delaware, Lackawanna and Western Railroad and played baseball on the side.
4. The Buffalo Bisons of the Eastern League.
5. The Boston Beaneaters, who still exist today as the Atlanta Braves.
6. $500
7. The Louisville Colonels.
8. $500
9. Fielding bunts. He was considered a pioneer because at the time shortstops would field bunts on the third-base side.
10. Putouts
11. Home runs with 15. In 1897 he also had a .346 batting average and knocked in 132 runs.
12. They offered him a position as the team's player/manager (which was common then). Along with a $5,500 salary, a $3,500 signing bonus and a cut of the team's profits.
13. He hit the franchise's first inside-the-park grand slam.
14. Chick Stahl
15. He committed suicide
16. The Philadelphia Athletics
17. Infielder John Knight
18. Hit a home run.
19. Collins spent 1909 with the Minneapolis Millers of the American Association, then spent two seasons with the Providence Grays in the Eastern League.
20. He was the first third baseman to be enshrined.

Joe Cronin

1. Where was Joe Cronin born on October 12, 1906?
2. What catastrophe had his parents just endured?
3. What baseball-related promotion caused his grades to rise as a youth?
4. Who is credited with discovering Cronin?
5. Who allegedly said about Cronin's signing, "You paid $7,500 for that bum? Well, you didn't buy him for me. You bought him for yourself. He's not my ballplayer, he's yours. You keep him and don't either you or Cronin show up at the ballpark."
6. Who did Cronin eventually marry?
7. With which team did Cronin break into the Major Leagues?
8. How old was he at the time?
9. True or false, in 1930 Cronin was the equivalent of the American League MVP before the award was created.
10. For which team was he named the player/manager in 1933?
11. How did the Red Sox acquire Cronin in 1935?
12. Who once said: "With a man on third and one out, I'd rather have Cronin hitting for me than anybody I've ever seen, and that includes Cobb, Simmons and the rest of them."
13. Why did Cronin urge the Red Sox to trade minor-league player Pee Wee Reese, who went on to a Hall of Fame career with the Brooklyn Dodgers?
14. How many times was Cronin named an All-Star?
15. True or false, Cronin finished his 20-year playing career with a batting average above .300.
16. How many times did he hit .300 or better?
17. How many times did he drive in more than 100 runs?
18. What job did Cronin hold after his playing and managing days ended?
19. Which legendary player did he pass on signing?
20. In 1959, Cronin was the first former player elected to hold what position?

Answers

1. San Francisco, California.
2. The San Francisco earthquake, which had cost them most of their possessions.
3. The San Francisco Seals of the Pacific Coast League began giving away tickets to students with good conduct and attendance records.
4. Joe Engel, one of the most eccentric promoters in baseball history who was also known for being one of the game's greatest scouts.
5. Washington Senators owner Clark Griffith.
6. Clark Griffith's niece, Mildred Robertson.
7. The Pittsburgh Pirates
8. 19
9. True. He batted .346, with 13 home runs and 126 RBIs.
10. The Washington Senators
11. They traded for him. He retired as a player in 1945, but remained manager of the Red Sox until 1947.
12. Connie Mack
13. Cronin realized while scouting Reese that he was watching his heir apparent with the Red Sox.
14. Seven, but he participated in 12 (including as a manager, coach and honorary captain).
15. True
16. Eight
17. Eight
18. He was the Red Sox' general manger from 1947–59.
19. Willie Mays. By January 1959 the Red Sox were the only team in the Major Leagues without a black player.
20. President of the American League

Bobby Doerr

1.   What was Bobby Doerr's full name?
2.   Where was he born on April 7, 1918?
3.   With what team did he begin his professional career?
4.   Which future teammate did Doerr first meet while playing for the minor-league version of the San Diego Padres in 1936?
5.   How old was Doerr when he broke into the Major Leagues?
6.   What statistical category did he lead the American League in 1938?
7.   Beginning in 1939, how many consecutive years did Doerr have at least 10 home runs and 73 RBIs?
8.   In 1940 the Red Sox became just the 12th team in Major League history to have four players with 100 RBIs. Which three players joined Doerr in that group?
9.   What statistical category did he lead the American League in 1944?
10.   Who edged Doerr for the batting title that season?
11.   Against what two teams did Doerr hit for the cycle?
12.   Why did Doerr miss the 1945 season?
13.   Who called Doerr "the silent captain of the Red Sox."
14.   What statistical category did he lead the American League in 1947?
15.   As a second baseman, what American League record did Doerr set in 1948?
16.   What statistical category did he lead the American League in 1950?
17.   How many times was he named an All-Star?
18.   True or false, Doerr appeared at positions other than second base during his 14-year playing career.
19.   Although he came back to baseball and filled many roles for the Red Sox, what did Doerr initially do after retiring as a player?
20.   With what corresponding move did Doerr resign from the Red Sox?

Bobby Doerr (left) is congratulated by his double-play partner, shortstop Johnny Pesky, after the game in which Doerr collected his 2,000th career hit.

Rick Ferrell

1. Where was Rick Ferrell born on October 12, 1905?
2. For which college did he play baseball and basketball?
3. How many brothers did he have?
4. True or false, they all played baseball at the major- or minor-league level.
5. With which organization did Ferrell originally sign?
6. True or false, Ferrell petitioned the Commissioner of Baseball, Kenesaw Mountain Landis, to make him a free agent on the basis that he was being unfairly held in the minors.
7. With which team did he make his Major League debut?
8. True or false, in 1931 he hit .306 and led all American League catchers in errors and passed balls, but also in assists.
9. Who else was involved in the trade that sent Ferrell to the Boston Red Sox in 1933?
10. That same season Ferrell was named to the first All-Star Game and was teammates with what familiar person?
11. Who did Ferrell hit a home run off of on July 19, 1933?
12. Who did the Red Sox sign in 1934, making a formidable battery partner for Ferrell?
13. To which team was Ferrell traded in 1937? (Bonus: Name the other players in the deal.)
14. True or false, at one point during his career Ferrell was catching for four knuckleball pitchers with the Washington Senators.
15. Why did Ferrell have such an impressive on-base percentage of .378?
16. True or false, he had a lifetime batting average of .300.
17. How many times was Ferrell named an All-Star?
18. For which organization did he serve as the general manager and vice president?

Answers

1. Durham, North Carolina
2. Guilford College
3. Six
4. False, only two of them did. Wes Ferrell reached the majors as a pitcher while George Ferrell was an outfielder in the minor league.
5. The Detroit Tigers
6. True
7. The St. Louis Browns
8. True
9. It was Ferrell and Lloyd Brown to the Red Sox in exchange for Merv Shea and cash.
10. His brother Wes. Rick Ferrell caught the whole game for the American League.
11. His brother Wes, who was with the Cleveland Indians. Wes hit a home run off Boston pitcher Hank Johnson, making it the first time in Major League history that brothers on opposing teams hit home runs in the same game.
12. His brother Wes, who in 1935 went 25–14 and finished second in American League MVP voting to Hank Greenberg.
13. The Washington Senators along with his brother Wes and Mel Almada for pitcher Bobo Newsom and outfielder Ben Chapman.
14. True: Mickey Haefner, Dutch Leonard, Johnny Niggeling, and Roger Wolff.
15. He was patient at the plate, with 931 walks compared to 277 strikeouts.
16. False, it was .281. He hit better than .300 four times.
17. Eight
18. The Detroit Tigers. The team won two World Series (1968 and 1984), and two American League Eastern Division titles (1972 and 1987) during his tenure.
19. Ray Schalk with 1,721. Ferrell ended up catching 1,884 games over 18 years.
20. Carlton Fisk in 1988.

20. Who eventually broke that record?

July 6, 1945?

19. Whose American League record for games caught did Ferrell break on

Carlton Fisk

1. Where was Carlton Fisk born on December 26, 1947?
2. Where did he attend college?
3. In what sport did he have a scholarship?
4. With what pick did the Red Sox take him in the 1969 draft?
5. In 1972, his first full season with the Red Sox, what offensive category did Fisk tie for the American League lead? (Bonus: Who did he tie?)
6. True or false, that was a career high for him.
7. In addition to American League Rookie of the Year, what other major award did Fisk win in 1972?
8. How many times did he win that award during his career?
9. In June 1974, who collided with him in a play at home plate, causing such knee damage that Fisk was told he would never play baseball again?
10. What was Fisk's batting average during the 1975 season, when he came back and played in 79 games?
11. How many times did Fisk drive in 100 runs with the Red Sox?
12. How many Silver Slugger Awards did he win during his career and how many were with the Red Sox?
13. Who was the Red Sox general manager who mailed Fisk a contract offer one day after the deadline?
14. How many times was Fisk named an All-Star?
15. When he retired in 1993, Fisk held the Major League records for most home runs by a catcher with 351 and most games played at the position with 2,226. Which two players broke them?
16. Which three New York Yankees in particular did Fisk have intense feuds with?
17. What number did Fisk wear with the White Sox?
18. Who was he almost traded for in 1985?

19. What was renamed in Fisk's honor during a pregame ceremony on June 13, 2005?

20. What team was the opponent and who caught his ceremonial first pitch that day?

Answers

1. Bellows Falls, Vermont
2. The University of New Hampshire
3. Basketball
4. Fourth overall
5. Triples with nine. He tied Joe Rudi of the Oakland Athletics.
6. True. He's also the last catcher to lead the league in that category.
7. A Gold Glove.
8. That was the only time.
9. Leron Lee of the Cleveland Indians.
10. .331
11. Once, 102 in 1977.
12. Three (1981, 1985 and 1988), all after he left the Red Sox
13. Haywood Sullivan
14. 11
15. Mike Piazza broke the home runs record and Ivan Rodriguez caught more games.
16. Thurman Munson, Lou Pinella and Deion Sanders.
17. 72, instead of 27. When he arrived Ken Kravec wore 27, and even though the pitcher was traded a few days later Fisk kept the uncommon number.
18. Don Baylor of the New York Yankees. A year later the Yankees traded Baylor to the Red Sox for designated hitter Mike Easler.
19. The left-field foul pole at Fenway Park
20. The Cincinnati Reds, who were making their first trip back to Fenway Park since 1975 for an interleague series, and former pitcher Luis Tiant.

Jimmie Foxx

1. Where was Jimmie Foxx born on Oct. 22, 1907?
2. Why did he drop out of high school early?
3. How old was Foxx when he made his Major League debut?
4. In 1929, when Foxx hit .354 and 33 home runs on what famous publication did he appear on the cover?
5. In 1932, why did Foxx have two home runs that didn't count, which would have given him 60 for the season and tied Babe Ruth's single-season record?
6. How did the Red Sox acquire him in 1936?
7. At that point how many consecutive seasons did Foxx have at least 30 home runs and 100 RBIs?
8. In 1938 Foxx had a career high in which major statistical category?
9. How many home runs did he hit that season?
10. What kept him from winning the triple crown?
11. True or false, Foxx had more walks than strikeouts during every season he played for the Red Sox.
12. What was the biggest salary Foxx made with the Red Sox?
13. What position did Foxx play for the first time in the majors during his final season?
14. Which two teams did Foxx play for after the Red Sox?
15. What uniform numbers did he wear for those teams?
16. How many home runs did Foxx have at the end of his career?
17. At the time, where was he on the all-time home runs list?
18. How many consecutive seasons did he hit 30 home runs?
19. Who eventually topped that?
20. Who was the first right-handed hitter to have more home runs than Foxx?

21. Who are the three other players in Major League history who hit 200 home runs with two different clubs?
22. Foxx is one of three players in American League history to have more than one six-hit game. Name the other two.

Former Red Sox great Jimmie Foxx (left) gives Red Sox rookie Harry Agganis a few pointers before a 1954 game at Fenway. (Frank Curtin)

Answers

1. Sudlersville, Maryland
2. To play for a minor league team managed by former Philadelphia Athletics standout Frank "Home Run" Baker.
3. 17
4. *Time*
5. The games were rained out and didn't count toward his statistics.
6. A's owner Connie Mack ran into financial problems during the Great Depression and sold off a number of his best players. After a 1936 contract dispute he sold Foxx' contract to the Red Sox for $150,000.
7. Seven
8. RBIs with 175.
9. 50, making him the first player to hit more than 50 home runs during a single season with two different teams.
10. Hank Greenberg hitting 58 home runs. Foxx lead the league with a .349 batting average and in RBIs.
11. False, but it was pretty close and his first and last seasons in Boston were the only ones in which he had more strikeouts than walks.
12. $27,500
13. Starting pitcher. He had made one appearance as a reliever with the Red Sox in 1939.
14. The Chicago Cubs and Philadelphia Phillies.
15. 16, 26 and 4
16. 534
17. Second behind Babe Ruth
18. 12, which was a Major League record
19. Barry Bonds in 2004.
20. Willie Mays in 1966.
21. Mark McGwire, Rafael Palmeiro and Manny Ramirez.
22. Doc Cramer and Kirby Puckett

Lefty Grove

1. What was Lefty Grove's real name?
2. Where was he born on March 6, 1900?
3. How old was he when he first played organized baseball?
4. With which team did Grove make his professional debut?
5. Which prominent independent minor-league team acquired him?
6. Which team finally purchased his contract and how much did it pay?
7. How many losing seasons did Grove have in the majors?
8. In 1928, Grove became the only pitcher in Major League history to do what?
9. Grove's 1931 MVP trophy is the only one not in the National Baseball Hall of Fame. Where is it?
10. In 1933, Grove became the first player in baseball history to do what as a batter?
11. What was involved in the trade that sent Grove to the Red Sox?
12. True or false, the only time during the first 13 years of his career that Grove didn't strike out at least 100 batters was his first season with the Red Sox.
13. How many times was Grove named an All-Star?
14. How many times did he lead the American League in ERA?
15. During which two seasons did Grove win the triple crown?
16. True or false, Grove had 55 saves over this career.
17. What did Grove do 298 times during his career?
18. True or false, Grove led the Red Sox to the World Series.
19. How many career wins did Grove finish with?
20. Among other pitchers with that many wins, how many have Grove's .680 lifetime winning percentage?

46 Red Sox Triviology

Answers

1. Robert Moses Grove
2. Lonaconing, Maryland
3. 19. He had primarily played sandlot ball.
4. The Martinsburg Mountaineers of the class-D Blue Ridge League.
5. The Baltimore Orioles, who then held on to him for four years while turning down numerous offers from Major League teams to buy his contract.
6. The Philadelphia Athletics paid $100,600, the highest amount for a player at the time.
7. One. His rookie year he had injury problems and finished 10–13.
8. Strike out the side on nine pitches twice during the same season.
9. George's Creek Library of the Western Maryland Regional Library system in Lonaconing.
10. Strike out five times in a nine-inning game.
11. Grove was traded along with Max Bishop and Rube Walberg, to the Red Sox for Bob Kline, Rabbit Warstler and $125,000.
12. True. Due to an arm injury he only made 12 starts.
13. Six (1933, 1935–1939).
14. Nine (1926, 1929–1932, 1935, 1936, 1938, 1939).
15. 1930 and 1931.
16. True.
17. Throw a complete game.
18. False
19. Exactly 300
20. No one

Harry Hooper

1. What's Harry Hooper's middle name?
2. Where was he born on August 24, 1887?
3. Why had his family migrated to that area?
4. Which college did he attend?
5. What did he have a degree in?
6. Name one of the two minor-league teams he played for before signing with a Major League organization.
7. His contract with one of those teams included side work doing what when not playing baseball?
8. Hooper was part of one of the best outfields in baseball. Who were the starting center fielder and left fielder?
9. In 1911, what was the combined batting average of that outfield?
10. In 1910, what two defensive categories did Hooper lead American League outfielders?
11. On May 30, 1913, Hooper became the first player in Major League history to do what double-dip?
12. Who were the pitchers involved in that?
13. Which two players have matched that accomplishment since then?
14. What team role was Hooper named to fill in 1919?
15. How many times did Hooper lead the American League in games played in right field?
16. How many times did Hooper lead the American League in putouts in right field?
17. How many times did Hooper lead the American League in assists in right field?
18. How many times did Hooper lead the American League in double plays turned from right field?

19. True or false, Hooper joined the 3,000-hit club.
20. After his baseball career was over, what position did he hold for 24 years?

Answers
1. Bartholomew
2. Bell Station, California
3. The California Gold Rush
4. St. Mary's
5. Engineering
6. The Oakland Commuters (1907) and Sacramento Senators (1908). Sacramento manager Charles Graham was a scout for the Boston Red Sox.
7. Railroad surveyor
8. Tris Speaker was the center fielder and Duffy Lewis was in left field.
9. .315
10. Assists (30) and errors (18)
11. He was the first player to lead off both games of a doubleheader with a home run.
12. Bob Groom and Walter Johnson of the Washington Senators
13. Ricky Henderson and Brady Anderson
14. Captain
15. Four
16. Six
17. Three
18. Three
19. False, he finished with 2,466.
20. Postmaster in Capitola, California.

Pedro Martinez

1. Where was Pedro Martinez born on October 21, 1971? (Bonus if you can spell it correctly.)
2. With which team did he initially sign and make his Major League debut?
3. What teammate said between them Martinez was the better pitcher?
4. Why was he primarily used as a reliever?
5. To which team was he traded, and for whom, before the start of the 1994 season?
6. True or false, Martinez won the Cy Young during his first season with the Red Sox.
7. What was so controversial about Martinez finishing second in MVP voting in 1999?
8. During the 1999 season, Martinez set the record for most consecutive innings pitched with a strikeout with how many?
9. True or false, during the 2000 season Martinez's combined ERA in his six losses was lower than the National League's Cy Young winner that season.
10. In 2000 Martinez' walks and hits per innings pitched (WHIP) was 0.74, setting a Major League modern record. Whose record did he break?
11. True or false, Martinez became the only starting pitcher in history to have more than twice as many strikeouts in a season as hits allowed.
12. Although Martinez led the American League in ERA, best WHIP, strikeouts, and winning percentage, who won the Cy Young Award?
13. True or false, Martinez won his only start against the Red Sox.
14. True or false, Martinez threw a no-hitter during his career.
15. Who was Martinez' victim for strikeout No. 3,000?
16. True or false, Martinez is the only pitcher in baseball history with at least 3,000 career strikeouts, but fewer than 3,000 innings pitched.

17. Who are the only two pitchers in Major League history to average more strikeouts per nine innings pitched?
18. What statistical accomplishment did Martinez achieve during the first inning on May 18, 2002?
19. Who were the batters involved?
20. True or false, Martinez' record with the Red Sox was the highest winning percentage any pitcher has had with any team in baseball history.

Pedro Martinez talks to the media after winning the 2000 American League Cy Young Award. (Charles Krupa)

Answers

1. Manoguayabo, Distrito Nacional, Dominican Republic
2. The Los Angeles Dodgers
3. Pedro's older brother Ramon Martinez.
4. Manager Tommy Lasorda thought Martinez was too small to be an effective starting pitcher.
5. Due to contract dispute with Jody Reed, the Dodgers sent Martinez to the Montreal Expos for Delino DeShields.
6. False. He finished second in the voting.
7. Martinez went 23–4 with a 2.07 ERA and 313 strikeouts. Although the Baseball Writers Association of America asked sportswriters to recuse themselves if they felt they couldn't vote for a pitcher; two left him completely off their ballots for that very reason (one of whom had previously voted for pitchers) and Martinez was edged by Texas Rangers catcher Iván Rodríguez.
8. 40
9. True. He had a 2.44 ERA in the losses, while Kevin Brown's ERA was 2.58.
10. Walter Johnson
11. True. He struck out 284 and gave up 128 hits.
12. Barry Zito. Martinez is the only pitcher since the Cy Young Award was created to lead his league in each of those four statistical categories and not win the award.
13. False. On June 28, 2006, Martinez lasted only three innings and gave up eight runs, six earned. The Red Sox are the only team he didn't record a win against.
14. False. Officially he didn't, although he had numerous near-misses including April 13, 1994, when he had a perfect game in the eighth inning and hit Reggie Sanders with a pitch, resulting in a brawl and his ejection, and June 3, 1995 when he took a no-hitter into the 10th inning.
15. Aaron Harang
16. True
17. Kerry Wood and Randy Johnson
18. The first known Immaculate Inning in Red Sox history, nine pitches, three strike outs.
19. Ichiro Suzuki, Mark McLemore and Ruben Sierra.
20. True. He was 117–37 (.759).

Johnny Pesky

1.   What's Johnny Pesky's original last name?
2.   Where did the Pesky name originate?
3.   Where was he born on February 27, 1919?
4.   With which NHL team did he once work out for?
5.   How was Pesky initially acquired by the Red Sox?
6.   During his first season with the Red Sox what rookie record did he set?
7.   In what statistical category did he also lead the American League?
8.   Who beat him out for the American League batting title?
9.   Who beat him out for American League MVP?
10. Why did Pesky miss the next three seasons?
11. What honor did Pesky receive for the only time in his career during the 1946 season?
12. What team record did he set in August 1946?
13. True or false, Pesky hit .300 every season he played for the Red Sox.
14. To which team was Pesky traded as part of a nine-player deal in 1952?
15. With which organization did Pesky begin his coaching career?
16. During his second stint as Boston's manager for five games in 1980, whom did he replace on an interim basis?
17. What number did Pesky wear as the team's manager in the 1960s?
18. What number did Pesky wear as a Red Sox coach from 1975–80?
19. What was named in his honor at Fenway Park?
20. How many home runs did he hit at Fenway Park?

Answers

1. Paveskovich
2. When he was in the minors his name was shortened to fit in the box sores. He legally changed it to Pesky in 1947.
3. Portland, Oregon
4. The Boston Bruins
5. He signed as an amateur free agent.
6. 205 hits
7. 22 sacrifice hits.
8. Ted Williams, Pesky hit .331, Williams .356.
9. Joe Gordon and Ted Williams
10. World War II
11. He was named an All-Star.
12. His 53 hits set the team record for hits in a month.
13. False, but he did so in six of the seven full seasons he played for Boston.
14. The Detroit Tigers
15. The New York Yankees
16. Don Zimmer
17. 22
18. 35
19. The right-field foul pole.
20. Six

Jim Rice

1. Where was Jim Rice born on March 8, 1953?
2. In 1975 Rice finished second in voting for the American League Rookie of the Year and third for MVP honors. Who finished ahead of him in both?
3. Why didn't Rice play in the 1975 postseason?
4. True or false, Rice never did win an MVP award.
5. What team record did he set in 1978?
6. In which of the following did he lead the American League: home runs, RBIs, hits, triples and/or slugging percentage?
7. In which of those same categories did he post career numbers?
8. Who is the only other player to lead the American League in total bases three straight seasons?
9. True or false, Rice is the only player in Major League history to have at least 200 hits and 39 home runs for three consecutive years.
10. From 1975–86, which of the following statistical categories did Rice lead the American League: total games played, at bats, runs scored, hits, home runs, RBIs, slugging percentage, total bases, extra-base hits, go-ahead RBIs, multi-hit games and/or outfield assists?
11. What Major League single-season record did Rice set in 1984?
12. Who did he tie for leading the league in this category in four consecutive seasons?
13. How many times was Rice named an All-Star?
14. In addition to 1978, in what other year was he the American League RBI champion?
15. How many times did Rice win a Silver Slugger Award?
16. How many times did Rice win a Gold Glove Award?
17. True or false, Rice finished his career with a batting average over .300.
18. True or false, Rice finished his career with a slugging percentage over. 500.

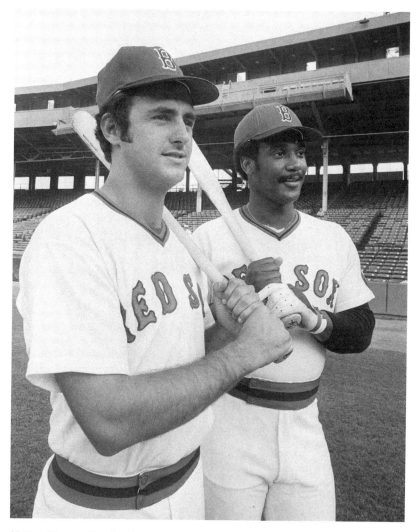

1975 rookie sensations Fred Lynn and Jim Rice ignited the Red Sox and helped take the team all the way to the World Series.

19. When was Rice finally elected to the Hall of Fame?
20. Only two other people were elected under similar circumstances. Name them.

1. Anderson, South Carolina
2. Teammate Fred Lynn won both awards. John Mayberry of the Kansas City Royals finished second in the MVP race.
3. A wrist injury after getting hit by a pitch.
4. False, he won it in 1978.
5. Total bases with 406, the most in the American League since Joe DiMaggio had 418 in 1937.
6. He led the league in all of them: 46 home runs, 139 RBIs, 213 hits, 15 triples, and .600 in slugging percentage.
7. All of them, although he tied the number of triples in 1979.
8. Ty Cobb
9. True
10. All of them.
11. Hitting into a double play, which he did 36 times.
12. Ernie Lombardi
13. Eight
14. 1983
15. Twice, 1983 and 1984.
16. Zero.
17. False. He just missed at .298.
18. True. He barely made it at .502.
19. During his 15th, and final, year of eligibility.
20. Ralph Kiner (1975) and Joe Medwick (1968) are the only other players to be elected during their final year of eligibility.

Carl Yastrzemski

1. Where was Carl Yastrzemski born on August 22, 1939?
2. Where did he initially go to college?
3. In what sport did he have a scholarship?
4. How much was his initial deal with the Red Sox?
5. True or false, after Yastrzemski signed his father bumped up his weekly allowance from $5 to $7.50 a week and he made him finish the semester at school.
6. At what school did he finish his degree a few years later, fulfilling a promise to his parents?
7. Who is the only other player in baseball history to play 23 years, all with one team?
8. When he won the Triple Crown in 1967, with whom did he tie for the American League lead in home runs?
9. Yastrzemski missed being a unanimous selection for American League MVP by one vote that year. Who got the other first-place vote?
10. On the final day of the regular season, when both the pennant and home run title were on the line, what did Yastrzemski do at the plate?
11. When he won the batting title in 1968, what was his average?
12. Before Yastrzemski hit 40 home runs and stole 23 bases in 1970, who was the only Red Sox to have a 40–20 season?
13. In May 1976, he tied the major league record of five home runs in two consecutive games. Who were the opponents?
14. How old was Yastrzemski when he hit his last home run? (Bonus: Name the opponent.)
15. Who is the only other player in American League history to collect over 3,000 hits and 400 home runs?

16. How many times was he named an All-Star?

17. In his autobiography *Yaz*, who did Yastrzemski say he would have stuck around to play with on the Red Sox had he known how good he was?

18. Who is the only Red Sox to win more Gold Glove awards than Yastrzemski's seven?

19. In which of the following statistical categories is Yastrzemski the Red Sox' all-time leader: at-bats, total bases, hits, games played, singles, RBIs, runs scored, doubles, grounding into double plays, or intentional walks?

20. True or false, Yastrzemski is the last batter in baseball to win a Triple Crown.

Answers

1. Southampton, New York
2. Notre Dame
3. Basketball
4. $108,000
5. True
6. Merrimack College
7. Brooks Robinson of the Baltimore Orioles.
8. Harmon Killebrew with 44 home runs.
9. Cesar Tovar, who finished seventh.
10. He went 4-for-4 with two RBIs as the Red Sox won 5–3 to clinch the pennant.
11. .301, the lowest average of any batting champion in Major League history. He was the only American League hitter that year to break the .300 mark, finishing well ahead of runner-up Danny Cater (.290).
12. Jackie Jensen, who did it twice (1954 and 1959).
13. He hit three home against the Detroit Tigers on May 19, and two against the New York Yankees the next day. All five home runs were hit on the road.
14. Yastrzemski was 44 years, 19 days old when he hit his last home run September 10, 1983, at Cleveland.
15. Cal Ripken, Jr.
16. 18
17. Roger Clemens
18. Dwight Evans with eight.
19. All of them. He's the all-time leader in at-bats (11,988), total bases (5,539), hits (3,419), games played (3,308), singles (2,262), RBIs (1,844), runs scored (1,816), doubles (646), grounding into double plays (323), and intentional walks (190).
20. False. Miguel Cabrera holds that distinction.

 **Cy Young**

1. What is Cy Young's real name?
2. Where was he born on March 29, 1867?
3. Why was he called "Cy?"
4. With which team did Young make his National League debut on August 6, 1890?
5. How did he do?
6. How much did Young get to jump from the National League's St. Louis Cardinals to play in the new American League?
7. True or false, Young won a pitching Triple Crown (leading the league in wins, strikeouts and ERA) during the American League's first season.
8. Who followed Young to the Red Sox?
9. Before the start of the 1902 season, which college did Young help as a pitching coach?
10. True or false, Young was a college graduate.
11. Who, after throwing a one-hitter against Boston on May 2, 1904, taunted Young and challenged the ace to face him in his next start?
12. How did Young respond when they faced each other?
13. Who snapped Young's streak of 25⅓ no-hit innings, including 76 batters, on May 11, 1903?
14. How old was Cy Young when he threw his third no-hitter?
15. How many seasons did he have 20 or more wins?
16. How many career wins did Young finish with?
17. True or false, on August 13, 1908, the league celebrated "Cy Young Day." No American League games were played on that day, and a group of All-Stars from the league's other teams traveled to Boston to play against Young and the Red Sox.
18. Who tied Young for career wins for the Red Sox with 192?

Answers

1. Denton True Young
2. Gilmore, Ohio
3. It's short for cyclone. The nickname came from the fences that he had destroyed using his fastball, because they looked like a cyclone had hit them.
4. The Cleveland Spiders.
5. He threw a three-hitter.
6. He got a $3,500 contract.
7. True. He was 33–10, with 158 strikeouts and a 1.62 ERA.
8. His favorite catcher, Lou Criger.
9. Harvard
10. False. Young stopped his formal education after he completed the sixth grade so he could help out on the family's farm.
11. Philadelphia Athletics pitcher Rube Waddell
12. He threw a perfect game, the only one in Red Sox history.
13. Sam Crawford of the Detroit Tigers with a single.
14. 41. He was the oldest pitcher to record a no-hitter until Nolan Ryan threw one at 43.
15. 15
16. 511
17. True
18. Roger Clemens
19. Brooklyn's Don Newcombe.
20. A statue by Northeastern University on the site of the Red Sox' original stadium, the Huntington Avenue Grounds.

19. In 1956, about one year after Young's death, the Cy Young Award was created. Who was the first recipient?

20. What was dedicated in Young's memory on September 23, 1993?

Seven

Jersey Numbers

Quick, the Boston Red Sox have never had a player on the roster with a last name beginning with what letter of the alphabet?

Considering that there have 1,742 different players, hailing from 24 countries through the 2015 season it's not that easy of a question. To try and put that in perspective 225 players have played for both the Red Sox and Yankees during their careers, plus 110 pitchers.

Nevertheless, only eight jersey numbers have been retired:

Number	Name	Date Retired
1	Bobby Doerr	May 21, 1988
4	Joe Cronin	May 24, 1984
6	Johnny Pesky	September 28, 2008
8	Carl Yastrzemski	August 6, 1989
9	Ted Williams	May 29, 1984
14	Jim Rice	July 28, 2009
27	Carlton Fisk	September 4, 2000
42	Jackie Robinson	April 15, 1997

It should be noted that the Red Sox didn't start wearing numbers on their uniforms until 1931, having played more than 30 years without them.

Also, the answer is "X," Boston has never had a player whose last name begins with an X. Next fewest is "I" with two, José Iglesias and Daryl Irvine. Perhaps that's what you get from a franchise that boasts the name Yastrzemski.

 # Jersey Numbers

1. Who was the first player to wear No. 1 for the Red Sox?
2. Bobby Doerr is best known for wearing No. 1, but when he was serving in the Army during World War II in 1945 two other players wore it. Name them.
3. Who was the last person to wear No. 1 for the Red Sox?
4. Who was the last player to wear No. 4?
5. Who wore No. 5 the longest?
6. Who last wore No. 6?
7. Who wore No. 7 as both a player and a coach?
8. Before Carl Yastrzemski wore No. 8 for the Red Sox, who wore No. 8 the longest?
9. Who wore Ted Williams' No. 9 during the 1944 season while he was serving in the military?
10. What number did Lefty Grove wear from 1934–41?
11. Which number has been worn by the most players as no one has sported it for more than seven seasons?
12. Who were the two players who wore it for seven seasons?
13. What number did Carl Crawford wear?
14. Who wore Jim Rice's No. 14 the most before he did?
15. Who wore No. 15 during the 2015 season?
16. Who was the first player to wear No. 64 for the Red Sox?
17. What two numbers did Johnny Pesky wear as a manager?

18. What number did Johnny Damon wear?
19. How about Fred Lynn?
20. Or Kevin Youkilis?
21. Which three people all wore No. 42 for the Red Sox on April 22, 2007 to honor the 60th anniversary of Jackie Robinson breaking baseball's color barrier?
22. Who was the last player to wear No. 42 on an everyday basis?
23. In 1934–35 the Red Sox had a player named Moose Solters, and we loved the idea of having a guy named Moose in the book so much, name one of the two numbers he wore for the Red Sox.
24. Who was the only player to wear No. 84?
25. Who was the only player to wear No. 99 for the Red Sox?

What number's hiding under that glove? (Charles Krupa)

Answers

1. Bill Sweeney in 1931.
2. Ty LaForest and Ben Steiner
3. Manager John McNamara
4. Carney Lansford
5. Nomar Garciaparra (1996–2004)
6. Gary Gaetti
7. Rick Burleson
8. Doc Cramer (1935–40)
9. Johnny Peacock
10. 10
11. 28
12. Steve Crawford and Doug Mirabelli
13. 13
14. Ike Delock
15. Dustin Pedroia
16. Dustin Pedroia in 2006.
17. 22 and 35
18. 18
19. 19
20. 20
21. Coach DeMarlo Hale, Coco Crisp and David Ortiz
22. Mo Vaughn
23. 5 or 22. His real name was Julius, so now you know why he went by a nickname. He played nine seasons in the American League for five different teams and had 3,421 plate appearances. He retired with a .289 career batting average. Sadly, in 1941 Solters was struck by an errant baseball during pregame warm-ups, which fractured his skull and caused him to go blind two years later.
24. J.T. Snow in 2006.
25. Through 2015 no one had worn it yet.

Eight

The Records

When it comes to records that the Boston Red Sox have set over the years, they could be a book by themselves.

For example, heading into the 2016 season Carl Yastrzemski is the all-time franchise leader in intentional walks with 190. The amazing thing is that Ted Williams is just sixth on that list with 86. (Note: He has the team record for "unintentional" walks with 2,021.)

Did you know that Yastrzemski was caught stealing 116 times, which is 52 more times than anyone else in Red Sox history. (Bobby Doerr had 64.)

Actually, for any question that begins with "Which hitter in Red Sox history had the most ..." Yastrzemski is a good guess.

Awards can be thrown in there as well, like Tim Wakefield and David Ortiz are the organization's only winners of the Roberto Clemente Award, and they did it in back-to-back years in 2010–11.

Bill Campbell and Tom Gordon are the only pitchers to win the Relief Man Award, in 1977 and 1998, respectively.

Heading into the 2016 season, the franchise's last home run champion was Tony Armas in 1984. John Dopson holds the Red Sox record in balks with 21.

You get the idea. It's difficult figuring out where to draw the line, like with "The Greats" section of this book that includes all of the players who have been inducted into the Hall of Fame who were primarily with the Red Sox, or had their jersey number retired (although an exception was made for Cy Young, 1901–08).

There are numerous other Hall of Fame players and coaches who were with the Red Sox at some point but are better associated with other teams. They include:

Luis Aparicio 1971–73
Lou Boudreau 1951–52
Jesse Burkett 1905
Orlando Cepeda 1973
Jack Chesbro 1909
Andre Dawson 1993–94
Dennis Eckersley 1978–84, 1998
Waite Hoyt 1919–20
Fergie Jenkins 1976–77
George Kell 1952–54
Heinie Manush 1936
Juan Marichal 1974
Herb Pennock 1915–22
Tony Perez 1980–82
Red Ruffing 1924–30
Babe Ruth 1914–19
Tom Seaver 1986
Al Simmons 1943
Tris Speaker 1907–15
Dick Williams 1963–64

Managers
Ed Barrow 1918–20
Lou Boudreau 1952–54
Frank Chance 1923
Hugh Duffy 1921–22
Bucky Harris 1934
Billy Herman 1964–66
Joe McCarthy 1948–50

The Records

1. Who has the Red Sox record for batting average by a rookie?
2. Who was the only player in the 20th century to record six errors during a game?
3. What's the team record of most rookie appearances during a single season?
4. In 1913 the Red Sox set an American League record for fewest home runs allowed in a season, which still stands. How many did they give up?
5. What's the Red Sox record for consecutive games played?
6. Who holds the Red Sox record for grand slams in a single season?
7. Who has the Red Sox record for doubles in a single season?
8. Which Red Sox has the most at-bats in a season without hitting a home run?
9. Who hit the most triples and stole the most bases in team history?
10. What's the franchise record for longest winning streak?
11. Who holds the single-season franchise record for putouts made by an outfielder with 503?
12. What's the franchise record for home runs by a rookie?
13. Who holds the Red Sox record for total bases in a single game?
14. Who holds the team single-season record for total bases?

15. What's the Red Sox record for times hit by a pitch during a season?
16. When Robert Clemens had a record 20 strikeouts against Seattle on April 29, 1986, how many batters did he walk?
17. How many of the Red Sox top 10 seasons in on-base percentage were by Ted Williams?
18. Who set a Major League record for most RBIs by a player who drove in all his team's runs in a single game?
19. What's the Red Sox record for most starts by a rookie during a season?
20. Who holds the Red Sox records for single-season and career leadoff home runs?
21. Who holds Boston's single-season record for home runs, and how many did he hit?
22. Who holds the Red Sox single-season record for home runs hit by a player age 21 or younger?
23. On April 22, 2007, the Red Sox hit a major league record four consecutive home runs against the New York Yankees. Who hit them?
24. Who is the only Red Sox player to have 30 home runs and 30 steals in a season?
25. What's the team record for most players used during a season?
26. Who has the longest winning streak by a pitcher during a season?
27. Who has the longest winning streak by a pitcher against one opponent?
28. Which pitcher holds the Red Sox record for strikeouts in a season?
29. Who holds the Red Sox record for most home runs by a third baseman in a single season?
30. Who is the only player in Red Sox history to have two pinch-hit grand slams?

Answers

1. Patsy Dougherty, who hit .342 in 1902. (Wade Boggs hit .349 in 1982, though he only had 338 at-bats.)
2. Shortstop Bill O'Neill made six errors during a thirteen-inning, 5–3 loss to the St. Louis Browns in 1904.
3. 1911 with 25. The most since 1926 was 19 in 2014.
4. Six.
5. Everett Scott with 832 from June 20, 1916 to Oct. 2, 1921. Scott ended up playing in 1,307 consecutive games, continuing the streak with the New York Yankees.
6. Babe Ruth with four in 1919.
7. Earl Webb with 67 in 1931.
8. Doc Cramer with 658 during the 1938 season. He also hit .301 and drove in 71 runs.
9. Harry Hooper
10. 15 games from April 25 through May 10, 1946.
11. Dom DiMaggio in 1948.
12. 34 by Walt Dropo in 1950.
13. Fred Lynn with 16, June 18, 1975 at Detroit.
14. Jim Rice with 406 in 1978.
15. 35 by Don Baylor in 1986
16. None. He gave up just three hits.
17. Nine. Wade Boggs had the 10th best season with a .476 on-base percentage in 1988.
18. Mike Greenwell with nine RBIs at Seattle on Sept. 2, 1996.
19. Nomar Garciaparra in 1997, 152 games.
20. Nomar Garciaparra hit seven in 1997, while Jacoby Ellsbury hit 10 during his Red Sox years
21. David Ortiz with 54 home runs in 2006.
22. Tony Conigliaro with 32 in 1965, one more than Ted Williams in 1939.
23. Manny Ramirez, J.D. Drew, Mike Lowell, and Jason Varitek.
24. Jacoby Ellsbury in 2011.
25. 56 in 2012.
26. Smokey Joe Wood, who won 16 straight starts in 1912
27. Ellis Kinder defeated the Chicago White Sox in 18 straight decisions from July 22, 1948– May 12, 1953.
28. Pedro Martinez with 313 in 1999.
29. Butch Hobson
30. Vic Wertz, in 1959 and 1960.

Nine

Quotes

Just about every big organization in professional sports has had a quote machine on the roster at some point, and for the Boston Red Sox no one compares to the pitcher known as "Spaceman," Bill Lee.

Lee pitched fourteen years in the Major Leagues (1969–1982), including 10 with the Red Sox, and went 119–90 with a 3.62 ERA.

Among his legendary quotes:

"You should enter a ballpark the way you enter a church."

"Baseball's a very simple game. All you have to do is sit on your butt, spit tobacco, and nod at the stupid things your manager says."

"You have two hemispheres in your brain, a left and a right side. The left side controls the right side of your body and the right side controls the left half. It's a fact. Therefore, left-handed pitchers are the only people in their right minds."

"Do you realize that even as we sit here, we are hurtling through space at a tremendous rate of speed? Think about it. Our world is just a hanging curveball."

"Do they leave it (the Green Monster) there during the game?"

"Hell, if KY Jelly went off the market, the whole California Angels pitching staff would be out of baseball."

"I'm mad at Hank (Aaron) for deciding to play one more season. I threw him his last home run and thought I'd be remembered forever.

Now, I'll have to throw him another."

"The other day they asked me about mandatory drug testing. I said I believed in drug testing a long time ago. All through the sixties I tested everything."

"I think about the cosmic snowball theory. A few million years from now the sun will burn out and lose its gravitational pull. The earth will turn into a giant snowball and be hurled through space. When that happens it won't matter if I get this guy out."

 # Quotes

Who said the following?

1. "Fenway is the essence of baseball."
2. "He has muscles in his hair."
3. "I was lucky enough to have the talent to play baseball. That's how I treated my career. I didn't think I was anybody special, anybody different."
4. "What very few batters knew was that I had two curves. One of them sailed in there as hard as my fastball and broke in reverse. It was a narrow curve that broke away from the batter and went in just like a fastball. The other was a wide break."
5. "He didn't have a curve. All he had was a fastball. Everybody knew what they were going to hit at, but they still couldn't hit him. He was fabulous."
6. "You know, a lot of people say they didn't want to die until the Red Sox won the World Series. Well, there could be a lot of busy ambulances tomorrow."
7. "It's a combination of both God-given ability and also hard work. I worked my butt off. You would never imagine the things I do, the things I used to do. In the Dominican, I used to run at 10:30 at night in the dark. I wasn't allowed to run in the day. The coach said, 'You are too skinny to run. You

need to build on weight.' So I ran in the dark field and there was a guard with a shotgun. I had to give him 20 bucks to let me run and be aware that I was there and not an intruder. Otherwise, in the dark of night you see somebody running and you shoot."

8. "I'd love to play in a Red Sox game. It would be so awesome to actually walk out on the field and play, just for one inning. I'd also steal everything I could get my hands on in the clubhouse, which is why they won't let me do it."

9. "As soon as I got out there I felt a strange relationship with the pitcher's mound. It was as if I'd been born out there. Pitching just felt like the most natural thing in the world. Striking out batters was easy."

10. "A player should try to get along without any stimulants at all. Water, pure cool water is good enough for any man."

11. "Boys, I just couldn't help it. It drove me to it."

12. "The guys who made up this schedule must have been in a room with a bottle of Wild Turkey and 40 straws."

13. "A baseball game is simply a nervous breakdown divided into nine innings."

14. "There is a lot of luck in baseball, and what is luck? Luck is really just a lot of practice and a lot of work. I think it goes back to bouncing the ball off the steps a jillion times and my God, pretty soon you have to get pretty good."

15. "He was a moody guy, a tantrum thrower like me. But when he punched a locker or something he always did it with his right hand. He was a careful tantrum thrower."

16. "They pick me [to be tested for steroids] every time. I don't know why. I don't know if it's because I'm a big guy, or what, but all I know is all they are going to find is a lot of rice and beans."

17. "As I grew up, I knew that as a building (Fenway Park) was on the level of Mount Olympus, the Pyramid at Giza, the nation's capitol, the czar's Winter Palace, and the Louvre—except, of course, that it's better than all those inconsequential places."

18. "Somebody had to make the decision for me because I wouldn't have done it. I would much rather have left like I've done today than to leave in the middle of the season or getting booed out of the ballpark. I didn't want to taint my career."

19. "Ten days you guys spend teaching me how to go up the hill and there isn't one of you with the brains to teach me how to come down again."

20. "If I knew it was worth that much after I missed it, I would've run after it."

21. "They can talk about Babe Ruth and Ty Cobb and Rogers Hornsby and Lou Gehrig and Joe DiMaggio and Stan Musial and all the rest, but I'm sure not one of them could hold cards and spades to (Ted) Williams in his sheer knowledge of hitting."

22. "There were seven of us kids and we ran out of m's."

23. "We picked the Red Sox because they lose. If you root for something that loses for 86 years, you're a pretty good fan. You don't have to win everything to be a fan of something."

24. "I don't know much about guns. I'm not Charlton Heston."

25. "I saw it all happen, from beginning to end. But sometimes I still can't believe what I saw: this nineteen-year-old kid, crude, poorly educated, only lightly brushed by the social veneer we call civilization, gradually transformed into the idol of American youth and the symbol of baseball the world over—a man loved by more people and with an intensity of feeling that perhaps has never been equaled before or since. I saw a man transformed from a human being into something pretty close to a god. If somebody had predicted that back on the Boston Red Sox in 1914, he would have been thrown into a lunatic asylum."

26. "I asked him my usual questions about all aspects of hitting. I like to get young hitters stirred up to find out what they really know. And he knew everything! He's really a brilliant kid."

27. "Numbers are irrelevant to me. They don't mean anything. I never liked them. I don't need a stat to tell me if I had a good game."

28. "I can't find a way to beat them at this point. What can I say? I just tip my hat and call the Yankees my daddy."

29. "I think about baseball when I wake up in the morning. I think about it all day. And I dream about it at night. The only time I don't think about it is when I'm playing it."

30. "He was what few of us ever become; he was exactly what he set out to be. He said he wanted to be able to walk down the street some day and have people say, 'There goes the greatest hitter who ever lived.' And if they don't say that, it's only because they don't know what they're talking about."

Over the years, David Ortiz has had his share of memorable quotes. (Kyodo)

Answers

1. Tom Seaver
2. Yankees pitcher Lefty Gomez about Jimmie Foxx
3. Carl Yastrzemski
4. Cy Young
5. Doc Cramer on Lefty Grove
6. Johnny Damon
7. Pedro Martinez on being so effective as a pitcher despite his size.
8. Denis Leary
9. Babe Ruth
10. Cy Young
11. Outfielder/manager Chick Stahl prior to taking carbolic acid to kill himself during spring training. What "it" exactly was remains a mystery.
12. Dave Bergman
13. Earl Wilson
14. Bobby Doerr
15. Ted Williams on Lefty Grove
16. David Ortiz
17. Bart Giamatti
18. Dennis Eckersley on retiring.
19. Smead Powell Jolley on the incline that used to lead up to the left field wall at Fenway Park. During his first game in 1932 he overran a fly ball and came back down the incline, falling flat on his face and getting hit on the head by the ball.
20. Bill Buckner after the ball that went through his legs during the 1986 World Series sold for $93,000.
21. Carl Yastrzemski
22. Jimy Williams on the correct spelling of his first name.
23. Jimmy Fallon on setting the movie *Fever Pitch* in Boston. The ending had to be rewritten when the Red Sox won the World Series.
24. Jimy Williams about radar gun readings.
25. Harry Hooper on Babe Ruth
26. Ted Williams on Red Sox shortstop Nomar Garciaparra
27. Nomar Garciaparra
28. Pedro Martinez
29. Carl Yastrzemski
30. Broadcaster Bob Costas on Ted Williams.

Ten

More Than 100 Years, More Than 100 Questions

    As part of the 100th Anniversary Celebration of Fenway Park in 2012, the All-Fenway Park Team comprising the greatest 40 Red Sox players and three managers was named and celebrated.

    According to the Red Sox website/media guide the team was voted on by fans, historians, front office staff, and the club's historical and archival consultants. Here are the three teams selected:

C	Carlton Fisk	RHP	Pedro Martinez
1B	Jimmie Foxx	LHP	Lefty Grove
2B	Dustin Pedroia	Closer	Jonathan Papelbon
RB	Wade Boggs	DH	David Ortiz
SS	Nomar Garciaparra	Manager	Terry Francona
LF	Ted Williams	PH	Bernie Carbo
CF	Fred Lynn	RP	Dave Roberts
RF	Dwight Evans		

First Reserves

C	Jason Varitek
1B	Mo Vaughn
2B	Bobby Doerr
3B	Mike Lowell
SS	Johnny Pesky
LF	Carl Yastrzemski
CF	Dom DiMaggio
RF	Trot Nixon
P	Roger Clemens
P	Luis Tiant
P	Tim Wakefield
P	Dennis Eckersley
P	Dick Radatz
Manager	Joe Cronin

Second Reserves

C	Rich Gedman
1B	George Scott
2B	Jerry Remy
3B	Frank Malzone
SS	Rico Petrocelli
LF	Jim Rice
CF	Reggie Smith
RF	Tony Conigliaro
P	Babe Ruth
P	Smoky Joe Wood
P	Curt Schilling
P	Bill Lee
P	Jim Lonborg
Manager	Dick Williams

More Than 100 Years

Here's a question for every year of Red Sox history:

1901: Who led Boston in home runs and RBIs during its inaugural season?

1902: What pitcher threw 41 complete games while making 43 starts?

1903: Who led the American League with 195 hits and 107 runs scored?

1904: How many shutouts did Cy Young have while leading the league and setting a career best?

1905: Who led Boston in home runs with six?

1906: What did Boston fail to do over a four-game span, from August 2–6, during three games with the Chicago White Sox and one with the Cleveland Naps?

1907: After Chick Stahl died, Boston had three managers during the season. Name one of them.

1908: What did the Detroit Tigers do in consecutive games against the Red Sox to establish an unusual Major League record?

1909: Who led the Red Sox with 50 errors, but contributed to nearly as many double plays?

1910: With the Red Sox leading the league with 43 home runs, which two players were first and second with 10 and eight, respectively?

1911: Who hit a grand slam in the 11th inning for a 13–11 victory over the Detroit Tigers and nullify the first career grand slam by Ty Cobb earlier in the game?

1912: Smoky Joe Wood led the league in complete games (35), wins (34) and shutouts (10). Which of those three was a career high?

1913: On July 3, the Red Sox set a record for most hits in a losing effort of a shutout with 15. Who was the opposing pitcher?

1914: Who pitched two complete-game victories for the Red Sox against the Detroit Tigers on Sept. 22, 1914?

1915: Who did Babe Ruth hit his first career home run off?

1916: Despite coming off a World Series title, which non-Major League team did the Red Sox lose to 1–0 in an exhibition game on April 2?

1917: Who led the American League with 35 complete games?

1918: Who started playing Babe Ruth as an outfielder/first baseman when he wasn't pitching?

1919: When Babe Ruth first broke the record for home runs in a single season, how many did he hit?

1920: Without Babe Ruth in the lineup, which players led the Red Sox in hits, home runs and RBIs?

1921: Who threw five shutouts, the most in the American League?

1922: Although the Red Sox finished last in the American League, in what team pitching category did it lead the league?

1923: What auspicious opening did the Red Sox participate in on April 18th and how did it turn out for them?

1924: Which team played one fewer game than the Red Sox, which kept Boston from finishing last in the American League?

1925: What Boston outfielder initiated three double plays against the St. Louis Browns on May 19?

1926: Which number was greater, wins by the first-place Yankees, or losses by the Red Sox?

1927: What future Red Sox hit his first career home run on July 18 for the Philadelphia Athletics?

1928: Who led the American League in stolen bases with 30?

1929: Which opponent had 29 hits while crushing the Red Sox 24–6 at Fenway Park on May 1?

1930: Who lost 20 games as a starting pitcher?

1931: Who topped the American League with 67 doubles?

1932: After Dale Alexander was acquired in a trade he went on to win the American League batting title with a .367 average. From which team was he traded?

1933: What did Babe Ruth do for the final time in his career while leading a 6–5 victory over the Red Sox on Oct. 1?

1934: What round number did Billy Werber have when he led the American League in stolen bases?

1935: While Wes Ferrell led the American League in wins (25) and complete games (31), which teammate had the best ERA at 2.70?

1936: Who had the biggest salary, Joe Cronin, Jimmie Foxx or Lefty Grove?

1937: On Dec. 6 the Red Sox announced they had acquired the contract of what 19-year-old prospect?

1938: What did Jimmie Foxx do six times against the St. Louis Browns on June 16?

1939: Who led the American League in RBIs with 145?

1940: Frustrated with the Boston media, who asked to be traded to the Detroit Tigers?

1941: When Ted Williams' pursuit of .400 came to an end, what was his final batting average?

1942: What was Ted Williams' batting average the subsequent season?

1943: From May 31 to June 2 the Red Sox and St. Louis Browns played four consecutive extra-inning games. How many total innings did they play?

1944: Although the Red Sox didn't have a player lead the American League in hits, home runs or wins, it had three different players top it in on-base percentage (.431), slugging percentage (.528), and winning percentage (.783). Name them.

1945: What did rookie pitcher Boo Ferriss do to get his career off to an impressive start?

1946: Who became the first player in American League history to score six runs in a game during a 14–10 victory against the Chicago White Sox on May 8?

1947: On July 20, the Red Sox participated in the first game in which two black players appeared in the same lineup, Willard Brown and Hank Thompson. What team did they play for?

1948: Who won the 17-inning spring training game between the Red Sox and New York Yankees on March 29th?

1949: Who led the American League with 25 wins, and what teammate topped it with a .793 winning percentage?

1950: What "first" did Billy Goodman achieve when he won the American League batting title with a .354 average?

1951: Who went 1-for-4 during his Major League debut against the Red Sox on April 17?

1952: Who was the only pitcher to face both Babe Ruth (1934) and Mickey Mantle (1952)?

1953: How many runs did the Red Sox score in the seventh inning to set a record on June 18? Bonus: Name the opponent.

1954: Which team completed an embarrassing 11 home-game sweep of the visiting Red Sox on August 30?

1955: At the beginning of the season the Red Sox were one of only three teams that still had yet to field a black ballplayer. Name the other two.

1956: Who threw the Red Sox' first no-hitter since 1923?

1957: How many times was Ted Williams intentionally walked to set an American League record?

1958: While Ted Williams led the American League in batting average and on-base percentage, who had the most RBIs?

1959: On July 21, the Red Sox became the last Major League team to have its first black player on its roster. Name him.

1960: Who did Ted Williams tie, and then pass, on the all-time home run list at 493?

1961: Which Red Sox pitcher did Roger Maris hit 61* off of?

1962: What American League first did Earl Wilson pull off with a 2–0 victory over the visiting California Angels on June 26?

1963: Although Carl Yastrzemski led the American League in numerous batting categories, total bases was not one of them. Who did?

1964: What two opposing pitchers struck out 17 Red Sox batters during a doubleheader at Fenway Park on September 30? (Hint: One would later be a well-known Red Sox.)

1965: What two headline-grabbing things occurred on September 16, when the Red Sox played the Cleveland Indians?

1966: Boston finished 72–90, 25 games behind the first-place Baltimore Orioles. What was the only American League team to finish lower in the American League standings at 70–89?

1967: What rookie had a no-hitter broken up with two outs in the ninth inning against the New York Yankees on April 14, and would only win two games the rest of his career?

1968: Who led the American League with 109 RBIs?

1969: Which opposing player hit two home runs and drove in a total of 10 runs to lead a 21–7 victory at Fenway Park on June 14?

1970: Carl Yastrzemski was by far the highest-paid player on the Red Sox. What was his base salary?

1971: Carl Yastrzemski signed what was believed to be the richest player contract in baseball history. How much was the three-year contract for?

1972: By playing an extra game, which team edged the Red Sox by a half-game to win the American League East?

1973: When Carlton Fisk and Thurman Munson of the New York Yankees squared off after Munson plowed into Fisk while trying to score from third on a missed bunt, who missed the bunt?

1974: Who threw seven shutouts en route to a 22–13 record?

1975: What unmatched double-awards accomplishment did Fred Lynn pull off?

1976: Who had the biggest salary on the Red Sox at $200,000?

1977: How many home runs did the Red Sox hit at Fenway Park to tie a Major League record on July 4th and end a nine-game losing streak?

1978: When the Red Sox and Yankees finished tied for first in the American League East, who hit a key three-run home run in the one-game playoff?

1979: Carl Yastrzemski reached two major milestones, 3,000 hits and 400 home runs, making him the first player in American League history to do both. Which did he achieve first?

1980: Which former Cincinnati Red, who faced the Red Sox in the 1975 World Series, was Boston's first baseman and hit 25 home runs?

1981: While Dwight Evans led the American League in total bases and walks, and tied for the lead in home runs, which teammate had the best batting average?

1982: Who hit .349 during his first season with the Red Sox, providing a strong glimpse of what was to follow?

1983: When Dave Righetti threw a 4–0 no-hitter against the Red Sox on July 4, the Yankees' third baseman was appearing in his 11th no-hit game. Name him.

1984: Who led the American League with 43 home runs, 123 RBIs and 339 total bases?

1985: What did catcher Rich Gedman do during a 13–1 victory over the Blue Jays on Sept. 18?

1986: What accomplishment was Roger Clemens the first starting pitcher to do since Vida Blue in 1971?

1987: Which 6-foot-5 rookie, who had been a first-round draft pick in 1982, did fans hope would become the Red Sox' next big bat in the lineup?

1988: True or false, in addition to finishing atop the East Division, the Red Sox also had the American League's biggest payroll.

1989: Who played the most games behind the plate for the Red Sox?

1990: What two fielding records did the Red Sox and Minnesota Twins set in back-to-back games?

1991: Which product of Mississippi State led the Red Sox with 28 home runs and 87 RBIs?

1992: Out of Boston's 73 wins, how many saves did Dennis Eckersley record?

1993: When former Red Sox catcher Carlton Fisk retired, he set the record for most total bases by a catcher. How many did he finish with?

1994: Who led the Red Sox with 26 home runs, 82 RBIs and 122 hits during the strike-shortened season?

1995: In what unique way did the Red Sox score all their runs during an 8–0 victory over the Yankees?

1996: Which former Red Sox who had played for four other teams died at the age of 100 and had played with more Hall of Fame teammates and managers, 18, than anyone in Major League history?

1997: Of the 24 pitchers the Red Sox used who was the only one who was shorter than 6-foot?

1998: Between starters Pedro Martinez, Bret Saberhagen, and Tim Wakefield, who had the most wins?

1999: When Pedro Martinez won the pitching triple crown by leading the American League in wins, strikeouts, and ERA, he became just the second pitcher in franchise history to do so. Who was the first?

2000: Who won his second straight batting title, this time with a .372 average?

2001: Which pitcher led the American League in strikeouts with 220?

2002: Who stole eight bases while appearing in 54 games for the Red Sox?

2003: Who led the American League in batting with a .326 average?

2004: Who struck out 177 times for the Red Sox?

2005: Who retired with a .295 batting average, 2,239 hits, 7,592 at-bats, two World Series titles, three Gold Gloves and one batting title?

2006: Although he had a much higher ERA, which starting pitcher beat out Curt Schilling for the team lead in wins with 16?

2007: Who went 238 games, a span that would go from July 5, 2006 to June 7, 2008, without making an error at first base to set an American League record?

2008: Who led the American League with 50 stolen bases?

2009: Who led the Red Sox in home runs (36) and RBIs (119)?

2010: The Red Sox had four players hit 20 home runs or more. Name them.

2011: Who led the Red Sox with 213 hits, edging Jacoby Ellsbury by just one to tie for the American League lead?

2012: Who was the opponent and what was the outcome when the Red Sox celebrated the 100th birthday of Fenway Park?

2013: What did Red Sox fans start to wear, both real and fake, in support of the team?

2014: After winning the 2013 World Series, in what place did the Red Sox finish in the American League East?

2015: Who did the Red Sox hire in a surprising front-office shakeup?

2016: What Red Sox legend announced before training camp that 2016 would be his last season?

1924: The Chicago White Sox, who went 66–87, while the Red Sox finished 67–87.
1925: Ira Flagstead
1926: The losses. Boston had 107 compared to 91 wins for New York.
1927: Jimmie Foxx
1928: Buddy Myer
1929: The Philadelphia Athletics
1930: The Red Sox actually had two pitchers with 20 losses. Milt Gaston was 13–20, and Jack Russell was 9–20.
1931: Earl Webb
1932: The Detroit Tigers
1933: Pitch. He also hit a home run in the game.
1934: 40
1935: Lefty Grove
1936: Jim Cronin at $27,000 a season.
1937: Ted Williams
1938: Walked in eight at-bats, to tie a Major League record.
1939: Ted Williams
1940: Ted Williams
1941: .406
1942: .356, which still won the American League batting title.
1943: 45
1944: Bob Johnson, Bobby Doerr and Tex Hughson.
1945: He set an American League record for most scoreless innings at the start of a career with 22. The Detroit Tigers snapped the streak on May 13.
1946: Johnny Pesky
1947: The St. Louis Browns
1948: No one. After 4 hours and 2 minutes of play the game was called, resulting in a 2–2 tie. It was the longest spring training game in Major League history.
1949: Mel Parnell and Ellis Kinder (23–6).
1950: He was the first batting champion who was not a regular position player. He played 45 games in left field, 27 at third base, 21 at first base, five at second base and one at shortstop.
1951: Mickey Mantle
1952: Al Benton
1953: 17 runs against the Detroit Tigers.
1954: The Cleveland Indians
1955: Detroit Tigers and Philadelphia Phillies. By 1958 the Red Sox would be the only team yet to have had a black player on the roster.
1956: Mel Parnell
1957: 33, but the American League only started keeping track of intentional walks in 1955.
1958: Jackie Jensen
1959: Pumpsie Green
1960: Lou Gehrig

1961: Tracy Stallard

1962: He was the first black pitcher to throw a no-hitter in the American League.

1963: Dick Stuart, who also led the league in RBIs.

1964: Luis Tiant and Sam McDowell. In the process the Cleveland Indians set an American League record for team strikeouts during a single season.

1965: Dave Morehead threw a no-hitter and was only a walk away from a perfect game, and General Manager Pinky Higgins was fired and replaced by Dick O'Connell.

1966: The New York Yankees

1967: Billy Rohr

1968: Ken Harrelson

1969: Reggie Jackson of the Oakland Athletics

1970: $125,000

1971: $500,000

1972: The Detroit Tigers were 86–70, and the Red Sox finished 85–70.

1973: Gene Michael

1974: Luis Tiant

1975: He was named both the American League's Rookie of the Year and Most Valuable Player.

1976: Pitcher Fergie Jenkins.

1977: Eight, while defeating the Toronto Blue Jays 9–6.

1978: Bucky Dent

1979: Carl Yastrzemski hit his 400th home run on July 24th, and career hit No. 3,000 on September 12th.

1980: Tony Perez

1981: Carney Lansford with a .336 batting average.

1982: Wade Boggs

1983: Bert Campaneris

1984: Tony Armas

1985: Hit for the cycle. He would never hit another triple after the 1985 season.

1986: Win both the Cy Young Award and the Most Valuable Player Award during the same season.

1987: Sam Horn

1988: False. The New York Yankees had a payroll of $21.5 million, while the Red Sox spent "just" $15.6 million.

1989: Journeyman Rick Cerone, who was best known for his years with the New York Yankees.

1990: The day after the Minnesota Twins turned two triple plays, the teams combined to hit into 10 double plays.

1991: Jack Clark

1992: 51

1993: 3,999. He also set the record for most games caught with 2,226, which had been previously held by Bob Boone.

1994: Mo Vaughn

1995: Grand slams by John Valentin and Mo Vaughn in consecutive innings. It's believed to be the only game to ever finish with two grand slams accounting for all of the runs scored.

1996: Milt Gaston

1997: Tom Gordon, who was 5–9 and would have a career-high 46 saves in 1998.
1998: Pedro Martinez with 19, but it was close. Tim Wakefield had 17 and Bret Saberhagen 15.
1999: Cy Young in 1901, 98 years previous.
2000: Nomar Garciaparra
2001: Hideo Nomo
2002: Ricky Henderson
2003: Bill Mueller
2004: Mark Bellhorn
2005: John Olerud
2006: Josh Beckett. He'd notch 20 wins in 2007.
2007: Kevin Youkilis. He also set the record for errorless games in a season by a first baseman with 135.
2008: Jacoby Ellsbury
2009: Jason Bay
2010: David Ortiz (32), Adrian Beltre (28), J.D. Drew (22), and Victor Martinez (20). Kevin Youkilis just missed with 19 home runs.
2011: Adrian Gonzalez
2012: The Red Sox played the New York Yankees and lost 6–2 on five home runs.
2013: Beards
2014: Last
2015: The Red Sox hired Dave Dombrowski for the newly created position of president of baseball operations on August 18, two weeks after his departure from the Detroit Tigers. Boston general manager Ben Cherington subsequently resigned.
2016: David Ortiz

Eleven

Drafts, Trades, and Free Agency, Oh My!

It's normal for a Major League Baseball franchise to make numerous personnel moves during a season and the Boston Red Sox are no exception.

For example, on December 1, 2015 (which was a completely random day other than it was when I turned in this manuscript), the Red Sox' 40-man roster was made up of 18 players who had been drafted by the organization, 12 who had been acquired in a trade, nine free-agent signings and one claimed off waivers.

Of course, only 25 can be active with the parent team at any one time and some of those drafted players will start 2016 in the minors, but you get the idea. Baseball teams are built in a variety of different ways, and here are some of the key transactions in Red Sox history:

Drafts, Trades, and Free Agency

1. How old was Cy Young when Boston traded him to the Cleveland Naps in 1908?
2. When the Red Sox traded away Tris Speaker, the 1912 American League MVP, what did they get in return?
3. What did the Yankees give up to get Babe Ruth in 1920?
4. What was Ruth's response?
5. Why?
6. Who did they get for Harry Hooper in 1921?
7. Who did the Red Sox trade prior to the 1939 season to make room for Ted Williams on the roster?
8. When the First-Year Player Draft was held for the first time in 1965, who was Boston's first selection?
9. To which team was he traded in 1971?
10. Who did the Red Sox draft with the 15th-overall pick in the 1971 draft?
11. True or false, Boston took Fred Lynn in the second round that year.
12. When Roger Clemens was a first-round selection in 1983, who was the first player selected in the draft?
13. Who did the Red Sox land in a trade with Seattle on August 19, 1986, while giving up shortstop Rey Quinones, right-hander Mike Brown, right-hander Mike Trujillo and outfielder John Christensen?
14. In what round did Boston draft Curt Schilling in the final January draft in 1986?
15. Who was part of the deal that sent him packing in 1988?
16. What did the Red Sox give up to get him back in 2003?
17. Who did Boston trade Mike Easler for on March 28, 1986?
18. Who did the Red Sox acquire from the Chicago Cubs on December 8, 1987 for Al Nipper and Calvin Schiraldi?

David Ortiz follows through on a home run during his days with the Twins.
(Steve Matteo)

19. Who did Boston select in the first round of the 1989 draft, 23rd overall?
20. Who did the Red Sox take with the seventh-overall pick in the 1993 draft?
21. True or false, the Red Sox have never had the first-overall selection in the draft.
22. Which infielder did Boston select with the 12th-overall selection in 1994?
23. Who did the Red Sox acquire from Seattle on July 31, 1997 for pitcher Heathcliff Slocumb?
24. Who did the Red Sox give up to get Pedro Martinez from the Montreal Expos in November 1997?
25. True or false, Boston signed David Ortiz as a free agent after the Minnesota Twins couldn't find a team willing to give anything up in exchange and released him.
26. Who were the two other teams involved in the four-team trade that sent Nomar Garciaparra to the Chicago Cubs on the 2004 trade deadline?
27. Which member of the Colorado River Indian Tribes did Boston take with its first-round selection in 2005?
28. Who did Boston select with the compensatory pick it was awarded for the 2005 draft for losing Pedro Martinez through free agency?
29. Who did the Red Sox acquire in a three-team deal on the trading deadline in 2008, when Manny Ramirez was sent to the Los Angeles Dodgers?
30. How many first-round draft picks did the Red Sox have in 2011?
31. Who did Boston trade to the Los Angeles Dodgers while unloading more than $250 million in salary obligations in 2012?
32. True or false, the Red Sox traded away the entire season-opening pitcher rotation at the 2014 trade deadline.
33. Which two players did the Red Sox sign as free agents prior to the 2015 season for approximately $180 million?
34. According to the Elias Sports Bureau, Yoenis Céspedes and Jon Lester, both 2014 All-Stars, were the first players since 1992 to be traded for each other in-season after being named an All-Star earlier in that year. Which two players highlighted that high-profile trade?

35. In November 2015 the Red Sox traded third baseman Carlos Asuaje, shortstop Javier Guerra, left-hander Logan Allen and center fielder Manuel Margot to acquire whom?

Answers

1. 41. He was coming off a season in which he won 21 games and posted the lowest ERA of his career, 1.26.

2. Speaker was traded by the Red Sox to the Cleveland Indians for Sad Sam Jones, Fred Thomas, and and$55,000 in 1916.

3. $100,000 and a loan with Fenway Park as collateral.

4. After receiving the news he sent a telegram to his agent saying: "Will not play anywhere but Boston. Will leave for the East Monday."

5. Ruth had invested in a cigar business in Boston and he wanted to be there to keep an eye on it.

6. Harry Hooper was traded to the Chicago White Sox in exchange for Shano Collins and Nemo Leibold.

7. Right fielder Ben Chapman to the Cleveland Indians.

8. Outfielder Billy Conigliaro, the younger brother of Tony Conigliaro (Swampscott, Mass.) High School.

9. The Milwaukee Brewers. It was considered a blockbuster deal with Ken Brett, Billy Conigliaro, Joe Lahoud, Jim Lonborg, Don Pavletich and George Scott all going to Milwaukee in exchange for minor leaguer Patrick Skrable, Tommy Harper, Lew Krausse and Marty Pattin.

10. Jim Rice

11. False, he was a second-round selection in 1973. Boston took shortstop Ted Cox in the first round that year. He ended up playing just 13 games with the Red Sox.

12. Tim Belcher by the Minnesota Twins. He ended up playing 14 years in the majors for seven different teams and had a career record of 146–140.

13. Outfielder Dave Henderson and shortstop Spike Owen.

14. Second

15. He and Brady Anderson were dealt to the Baltimore Orioles for Mike Boddicker.

16. Jorge de la Rosa, Casey Fossum, Mike Goss, and Brandon Lyon.

17. Don Baylor

18. Lee Smith

19. Mo Vaughn

20. Trot Nixon

21. True. The best pick it ever had was third in 1967, when Boston took pitcher Mike Garman.

22. Nomar Garciaparra.

23. Catcher Jason Varitek and right-hander Derek Lowe.

24. Carl Pavano and Tony Armas, Jr.

25. True

26. The Minnesota Twins and Montreal Expos. The Red Sox received shortstop Orlando Cabrera from the Expos and first baseman Doug Mientkiewicz from Twins while sending shortstop Nomar Garciaparra and outfielder Matt Murton to the Cubs.
27. Jacoby Ellsbury with the 23rd-overall selection. His mother Margie is full-blooded Navajo.
28. Clay Buchholtz
29. Outfielder Jason Bay from the Pittsburgh Pirates.
30. Four, due in part to having compensation picks for losing free agents Victor Martinez and Adrian Beltre. It took Matt Barnes, RHP, Connecticut; Blake Swihart, C, V. Sue Cleveland HS in New Mexico; Henry Owens, LHP, Edison HS in California; and Jackie Bradley, OF, South Carolina. Incidentally, Swihart won a national wrestling championship at the age of nine and his father, Arlan, is a nuclear physicist.
31. First baseman Adrian Gonzalez, outfielder Carl Crawford, right-hander Josh Beckett and infielder Nick Punto. The Red Sox received right-hander Rubby De La Rosa, right-hander Allen Webster, first baseman James Loney, outfielder/first baseman Jerry Sands and infielder Ivan DeJesus.
32. False, but it came close. Jon Lester, John Lackey, Jake Peavy and Felix Doubront were all traded away. The four had started 72 of Boston's 108 games before the July 31st trading deadline.
33. Pablo Sandoval and Hanley Ramirez.
34. The Oakland Athletics sent Jose Canseco to the Texas Rangers for Ruben Sierra and two other players.
35. Closer Craig Kimbrel of the San Diego Padres.

Twelve

Opening Day Lineups

When it comes to baseball trivia there's nothing like an Opening Day lineup.

It's when the newest players first appear, departures become more real and the changes over the offseason take hold. Among pitchers it's when the staff ace usually takes his rightful place and begins what's hopefully the long march toward the playoffs.

For some reason fans can remember and recite Opening Day lineups until their dying day even though it could look different with each passing game. More than an annual benchmark, it's like a progress report, and no one ever remembers who started the second game of a 162-game season.

Opening Day Lineups

See how many of these 25 seasons you can peg the Opening Day lineup:

1. 1901
2. 1903
3. 1912
4. 1915
5. 1916
6. 1918
7. 1930
8. 1946
9. 1955
10. 1967
11. 1975
12. 1986
13. 1988
14. 1990
15. 1995
16. 1998
17. 1999
18. 2003
19. 2004
20. 2005
21. 2007
22. 2008
23. 2009
24. 2013
25. 2015

How many Opening Day lineups has Xander Boegarts been a part of? (Chris Szagola)

Answers

1. **1901**
   Tommy Dowd, LF
   Charlie Hemphill, RF
   Chick Stahl, CF
   Jimmy Collins, 3B
   Buck Freeman, 1B
   Freddy Parent, SS
   Hobe Ferris, 2B
   Lou Criger, C
   Win Kellum, P

2. **1903**
   Patsy Dougherty, LF
   Jimmy Collins, 3B
   Chick Stahl, CF
   Buck Freeman, RF
   Freddy Parent, SS
   Candy LaChance, 1B
   Hobe Ferris, 2B
   Duke Farrell, C
   George Winter, P

3. **1912**
   Harry Hooper, RF
   Steve Yerkes, 2B
   Tris Speaker, CF
   Jake Stahl, 1B
   Larry Gardner, 3B
   Duffy Lewis, LF
   Heinie Wagner, SS
   Les Nunamaker, C
   Buck O'Brien, P

4. **1915**
   Harry Hooper, RF
   Heinie Wagner, 2B
   Tris Speaker, CF
   Duffy Lewis, LF
   Dick Hoblitzel, 1B
   Everett Scott, SS
   Larry Gardner, 3B
   Hick Cady, C
   Ernie Shore, P

5. **1916**
   Harry Hooper, RF
   Everett Scott, SS
   Dick Hoblitzel, 1B
   Tilly Walker, CF
   Chick Shorten, LF
   Larry Gardner, 3B
   Jack Barry, 2B
   Pinch Thomas, C
   Babe Ruth, P

6. **1918**
   Harry Hooper, RF
   Dave Shean, 2B
   Amos Strunk, CF
   Dick Hoblitzel, 1B
   Stuffy McInnis, 3B
   George Whiteman, LF
   Everett Scott, SS
   Sam Agnew, C
   Babe Ruth, P

7. **1930**
   Jack Rothrock, RF
   Otto Miller, 3B
   Tom Oliver, CF
   Russ Scarritt, LF
   Bill Regan, 2B
   Phil Todt, 1B
   Bill Narleski, SS
   Johnnie Heving, C
   Danny MacFayden, P

8. **1946**
   Dom DiMaggio, CF
   Johnny Pesky, SS
   Ted Williams, LF
   Bobby Doerr, 2B
   Rudy York, 1B
   Catfish Metkovich, RF
   Ernie Andres, 3B
   Hal Wagner, C
   Tex Hughson, P

9. **1955**
   Billy Goodman, 2B
   Eddie Joost, SS
   Faye Throneberry, LF
   Jackie Jensen, RF
   Sammy White, C
   Norm Zauchin, 1B
   Ted Lepcio, 3B
   Jimmy Piersall, CF
   Frank Sullivan, P
10. **1967**
    José Tartabull, CF
    Joe Foy, 3B
    Carl Yastrzemski, LF
    Tony Conigliaro, RF
    George Scott, 1B
    Reggie Smith, 2B
    Rico Petrocelli, SS
    Mike Ryan, C
    Jim Lonborg, P
11. **1975**
    Juan Beníquez, LF
    Fred Lynn, CF
    Carl Yastrzemski, 1B
    Tony Conigliaro, DH
    Rico Petrocelli, 3B
    Dwight Evans, RF
    Bob Montgomery, C
    Rick Burleson, SS
    Doug Griffin, 2B
    Luis Tiant, P
12. **1986**
    Dwight Evans, RF
    Wade Boggs, 3B
    Bill Buckner, 1B
    Jim Rice, LF
    Don Baylor, DH
    Rich Gedman, C
    Tony Armas, CF
    Marty Barrett, 2B
    Glenn Hoffman, SS
    Bruce Hurst, P

13. **1988**
    Brady Anderson, CF
    Marty Barrett, 2B
    Wade Boggs, 3B
    Jim Rice, LF
    Mike Greenwell, RF
    Dwight Evans, 1B
    Sam Horn, DH
    Rich Gedman, C
    Spike Owen, SS
    Roger Clemens, P
14. **1990**
    Wade Boggs, 3B
    Marty Barrett, 2B
    Mike Greenwell, LF
    Ellis Burks, CF
    Dwight Evans, DH
    Billy Jo Robidoux, 1B
    Tony Peña, C
    Jody Reed, SS
    Kevin Romine, RF
    Roger Clemens, P
15. **1995**
    Luis Alicea, 2B
    John Valentin, SS
    José Canseco, DH
    Mo Vaughn, 1B
    Mark Whiten, RF
    Mike Greenwell, LF
    Mike MacFarlane, C
    Tim Naehring, 3B
    Lee Tinsley, CF
    Aaron Sele, P
16. **1998**
    Nomar Garciaparra, SS
    John Valentin, 3B
    Mo Vaughn, 1B
    Reggie Jefferson, DH
    Troy O'Leary, LF
    Scott Hatteberg, C
    Darren Lewis, CF
    Darren Bragg, RF

Donnie Sadler, 2B
Pedro Martínez, P
17. **1999**
José Offerman, DH
Darren Lewis, CF
John Valentin, 3B
Nomar Garciaparra, SS
Troy O'Leary, LF
Mike Stanley, 1B
Scott Hatteberg, C
Jeff Frye, 2B
Trot Nixon, RF
Pedro Martínez, P
18. **2003**
Johnny Damon, CF
Todd Walker, 2B
Nomar Garciaparra, SS
Manny Ramírez, LF
Kevin Millar, 1B
Shea Hillenbrand, 3B
Jeremy Giambi, DH
Trot Nixon, RF
Jason Varitek, C
Pedro Martínez, P
19. **2004**
Johnny Damon, CF
Bill Mueller, 3B
David Ortiz, DH
Manny Ramírez, LF
Kevin Millar, 1B
Gabe Kapler, RF
Jason Varitek, C
Mark Bellhorn, 2B
Pokey Reese, SS
Pedro Martínez, P
20. **2005**
Johnny Damon, CF
Edgar Rentería, SS
Manny Ramírez, LF
David Ortiz, DH
Kevin Millar, 1B
Jason Varitek, C

Jay Payton, RF
Bill Mueller, 3B
Mark Bellhorn, 2B
David Wells, P
21. **2007**
Julio Lugo, SS
Kevin Youkilis, 1B
David Ortiz, DH
Manny Ramírez, LF
J. D. Drew, RF
Mike Lowell, 3B
Jason Varitek, C
Coco Crisp, CF
Dustin Pedroia, 2B
Curt Schilling, P
22. **2008**
Dustin Pedroia, 2B
Kevin Youkilis, 1B
David Ortiz, DH
Manny Ramírez, LF
Mike Lowell, 3B
Brandon Moss, RF
Jason Varitek, C
Jacoby Ellsbury, CF
Julio Lugo, SS
Daisuke Matsuzaka, P
23. **2009**
Jacoby Ellsbury, CF
Dustin Pedroia, 2B
David Ortiz, DH
Kevin Youkilis, 1B
J. D. Drew, RF
Jason Bay, LF
Mike Lowell, 3B
Jed Lowrie, SS
Jason Varitek, C
Josh Beckett, P
24. **2013**
Jacoby Ellsbury, CF
Shane Victorino, RF
Dustin Pedroia, 2B
Mike Napoli, 1B

Will Middlebrooks, 3B
Jonny Gomes, DH
Jarrod Saltalamacchia, C
Jackie Bradley, Jr., LF
José Iglesias, SS
Jon Lester, P
25. **2015**
Mookie Betts, CF
Dustin Pedroia, 2B
David Ortiz, 1B
Hanley Ramírez, LF
Pablo Sandoval, 3B
Shane Victorino, RF
Xander Bogaerts, SS
Ryan Hanigan, C
Clay Buchholz, P

Thirteen

The Postseason

1903

1. Why was the series best of nine games?
2. Who threw a six-hitter in Game 1?
3. Who hit the first home run in World Series history?
4. True or false, that was the only home run his team would hit in the series.
5. Who threw a three-hitter in Game 2?
6. Who hit two home runs for Boston in Game 2?
7. Why did Pittsburgh have to use the same starting pitcher in Games 3 and 4?
8. True or false, it won both games anyway.
9. Who bounced back from a Game 1 loss to get the win in Game 5?
10. What was Boston's theme song, which its fans would sing to try to distract the opposing players?
11. Who took the loss in Game 7?
12. Who had a two-run single to set the tone in Game 8?
13. True or false, Pittsburgh had a better batting average in the series?
14. Why did the Pittsburgh players get paid more than their winning counterparts?
15. Who made the final out of the series?

Answers

1. There was no formal agreement in place for the league champions to meet so the owners, Pittsburgh's Barney Dreyfuss and Boston's Henry Killilea, agreed to do so and play a nine-game series. It was considered the first step in reconciling the feud between the leagues.
2. Pittsburgh's Deacon Phillippe, as it won 7–3.
3. Pittsburgh right fielder Jimmy Sebring.
4. True
5. Boston's Bill Dineen.
6. Patsy Dougherty
7. Sam Leever had a sore arm and 16-game winner Ed Doheny had arm problems that were made worse by entering a trapshooting competition. He left the team in mid-September, exhibiting signs of paranoia, and was eventually committed to an insane asylum.
8. True. Deacon Phillippe won both games and improved to 3–0 in the series, all complete games.
9. Cy Young.
10. "Tessie," Boston's "Royal Rooters" fans traveled to Exposition Park, where the visiting team won three out of four games.
11. Pittsburgh's Deacon Phillippe
12. Hobe Ferris
13. False. Boston batted .252 while Pittsburgh hit .237.
14. Pirates owner Barney Dreyfuss added his share of the gate receipts to the players' cut.
15. National League batting champion Honus Wagner, who struck out.

 **1912**

1. Who was New York Giants manager John McGraw's surprise starter in Game 1?
2. Did it pay off?
3. Which team won Game 2?
4. With the tying run at second base and two outs in the ninth inning, who caught Hick Cady's line drive to right with his bare hand when he missed it with his glove?
5. Who helped his cause with an RBI-single to bring in an insurance run during the 3–1 victory in Game 4?
6. What rookie pitcher started and won Game 5 and who did he beat?
7. Who got shelled for five runs in the first inning of Game 6?
8. Who made the decision for him to start that game?
9. What starting pitcher got pounded in Game 7, throwing just 13 pitches and recording one out on a sacrifice, to take the loss?
10. How was the location of Game 8, which hadn't originally been scheduled, determined?
11. What was the eyebrow-raising pitching matchup?
12. How did the Giants break a 1–1 tie in the 10th inning?
13. Who dropped a fly ball to allow the leadoff batter on base in the bottom of the 10th?
14. Who knocked in the tying run after three Giants allowed a foul ball to drop between them?
15. With the bases loaded and one out, who hit a sacrifice fly to bring in the series-deciding run?

Answers

1. Rookie Jeff Tesreau, who led the National League with an ERA of 1.96, over Christy Mathewson and Rube Marquard, who had gone undefeated in his first nineteen starts.
2. Nope. Boston ace Smoky Joe Wood led a 4–3 victory.
3. Neither. The game was called due to darkness tied 6–6 after 11 innings.
4. Josh Devore
5. Smoky Joe Wood
6. Hugh Bedient as Boston beat New York and Christy Mathewson, 2–1.
7. Buck O'Brien
8. Owner Jimmy McAleer overruled manager Jake Stahl, who wanted to start Smoky Joe Wood. Already upset that they wouldn't be getting a bigger cut for playing an extra game, Red Sox players believed their own front office was trying to extend the series to get more box office receipts.
9. Smoky Joe Wood
10. Coin flip. Boston won and hosted.
11. Boston's Hugh Bedient vs. New York's Christy Mathewson
12. Red Murray knocked a one-out double and scored on a Fred Merkle single off Smoky Joe Wood in relief.
13. Fred Snodgrass. It was later called "the $30,000 muff" as that was the difference in total payout. Each winning player's share was $4,025, while the losing players received $2,566.
14. Tris Speaker
15. Larry Gardner

 **1915**

1. Who made his World Series debut as a pinch-hitter in Game 1, and would spend the rest of the series on the bench?
2. Who was the winning pitcher in Game 1?
3. Who did he beat, 3–1?
4. How long would it take the Phillies to win another postseason game?
5. Who threw out he ceremonial pitch before Game 2?
6. Who held the Phillies to three hits and drove in the winning run in the ninth inning of Game 2?
7. Who retired the last 20 batters he faced en route to a 2–1 victory in Game 3?
8. Who drove in Harry Hooper in the ninth for the game-winning run?
9. Who allowed just seven hits in Game 4 as Boston won again 2–1?
10. Who hit a game-tying two-run home run in the eighth inning of Game 5?
11. Who hit two home runs, including game-winner in the ninth inning?
12. True or false, both of his home runs took advantage of the fence being moved in for more seating and today would have been ground-rule doubles.
13. True or false, those three were the only home runs of the series.
14. Who was the winning pitcher of Game 5, which had a 5–4 score?
15. True or false, despite being outscored just 12–10 in the series, the Phillies out-hit the Red Sox.

Answers

1. Babe Ruth
2. Philadelphia's Grover Cleveland Alexander, who had won 31 games during the regular season.
3. Ernie Shore
4. Until 1977
5. Woodrow Wilson, the first U.S. President to attend a World Series game.
6. Rube Foster
7. Left-hander "Dutch" Leonard
8. Duffy Lewis
9. Ernie Shore
10. Duffy Lewis
11. Harry Hooper
12. True
13. True
14. Rube Foster
15. False. The Phillies were out-hit 42–27.

1916

1. Between Boston and Brooklyn, which team was favored to win the World Series?
2. Who gave up four runs in the ninth inning, but with Carl Mays getting the save won Game 1?
3. Who hit an inside-the-park home run in the first inning of Game 2?
4. Who drove in a run in the third inning and threw 13 scoreless innings to eventually get the win?
5. Who got the key leadoff walk in the 14th inning?
6. Who eventually knocked in the game-winning run?
7. Who took the loss in the double masterpiece?
8. Game 3 was the first World Series game in what famous stadium?
9. Who chased Brooklyn starter Jack Coombs out of the game with a home run in the seventh inning?
10. Who was the winning pitcher of Game 3?
11. Who recorded the final eight outs to earn the save?
12. Who hit a three-run inside-the-park home run in Game 4 to win the game for Boston?
13. How fast was Game 5 played?
14. Which future manager led off the Dodgers ninth with a hit?
15. How much money did each winning player receive after the World Series?

Answers

1. Brooklyn, which boasted 25-game winner Jeff Pfeffer and acquired veteran pitchers Rube Marquard and Jack Coombs.
2. Ernie Shore
3. Hy Myers
4. Babe Ruth
5. Dick Hoblitzell
6. Del Gainor
7. Sherry Smith
8. Ebbets Field
9. Larry Gardner
10. Dutch Leonard
11. Jeff Pfeffer
12. Larry Gardner
13. 1 hour, 43 minutes
14. Casey Stengel
15. $3,910

1918

1. Why was the Fall Classic played in early September?
2. Where did the Cubs play their home games in the World Series?
3. What tradition was first observed during Game 1?
4. In Game 1, who extended his postseason scoreless innings streak to 22 while earning the win?
5. Who knocked in the only run of the game?
6. Who gave up just six hits while getting the win in Game 2?
7. Who got caught in a rundown between third and home while trying to score on a passed ball for the final out of Game 3?
8. Who threw 27 innings in the series and gave up just three runs, for a 1.00 ERA, but went 1–2?
9. Which team had a better batting average in the series?
10. What would happen first, the two teams in the 1918 World Series would play again or one of the teams would win another World Series?
11. Babe Ruth is the only starting pitcher in World Series history to do what?
12. How many runs did the Red Sox score in the series?
13. Who was the first pitcher in World Series history to walk 11 batters in a six-game series?
14. The 1918 World Series was the last one to not include what?
15. The threat of what loomed over the series and fed accusations later on that were never proven?

Answers

1. The regular season was shortened and ended on Labor Day due to World War I.
2. Comiskey Park due to its larger seating capacity.
3. The "The Star Spangled Banner" was performed for the first time at a Major League game. It was played during the seventh inning and would be declared the national anthem in 1931.
4. Babe Ruth
5. Stuffy McInnis
6. Lefty Tyler
7. Charlie Pick
8. Hippo Vaughn
9. The Cubs, even though they hit a horrendous .210 in the series. The Red Sox batted just .186.
10. The teams wouldn't meet again for 87 years until 2005, one year after the Red Sox broke the "Curse of the Bambino" by winning the 2004 World Series.
11. Not hit last in the batting order. In Game 4 he hit sixth.
12. Just nine, the fewest runs by the winning team in World Series history.
13. Lefty Tyler. He's since been matched by Lefty Gomez (1936), and Allie Reynolds (1951), but never surpassed.
14. A home run. The only other three to not have at least one were played in 1905, 1906 and 1907.
15. A player's strike due to low gate receipts. During the investigation of the 1919 Black Sox Scandal it was alleged that the Cubs threw the series to make up for their financial losses.

1946

1. Who did the St. Louis Cardinals beat in the first playoff to decide a pennant, a best-of-three series?
2. Who hit a home run in the 10th inning to give Boston a 3–2 victory in Game 1?
3. Who was the winning pitcher in Game 2, a 3–0 victory for the Cardinals?
4. Who threw a shutout in Game 3 to put Boston back out in front in the series?
5. Game 4 is the only game in World Series history in which three players on the same team all had four or more hits. Name them. (Hint: They all played for the Cardinals.)
6. Who had his only RBI of the series with a run-scoring single in Game 5?
7. What starting pitcher was chased in the third inning of Game 6, when he gave up three runs in a 4–1 loss?
8. Who hit a two-run double for Boston in the eighth inning to tie Game 7 up 3–3?
9. Who ignored third base coach Mike González' stop sign and scored from first base on the play called the "Mad Dash"?
10. Who hit .409 (9-for-22) for Boston, with a two-run home run, but only scored one run?

Answers

1. The Brooklyn Dodgers
2. Rudy York
3. Harry Brecheen
4. Dave Ferriss
5. Enos Slaughter, Whitey Kurowski and rookie catcher Joe Garagiola.
6. Ted Williams
7. Mickey Harris
8. Dom DiMaggio
9. Enos Slaughter on what was officially scored a double by Harry Walker. It turned out to be the winning run in a dramatic 4–3 victory.
10. Second baseman Bobby Doerr.

1967

1. What's the 1967 Red Sox season commonly called?
2. Who set the tone for the series by winning Game 1, 2–1, and threw a five-hitter in Game 4?
3. Who brought in both runs for the Cardinals in Game 1 with ground outs?
4. Who allowed just one total run in his complete-game wins for Boston in Game 2 and Game 5?
5. Who broke up his bid for a no-hitter with a double in the eighth inning?
6. Who hit two home runs in Game 2 for the Red Sox?
7. Who hit a key two-run home run for St. Louis to help lead a 5–2 victory in Game 3?
8. Which two Cardinals had two RBIs each in Game 4?
9. Boston hit three home runs in the fourth inning of Game 6, en route to an 8–4 victory. Who hit them?
10. Who allowed three hits while striking out 10 and hit a home run in Game 7?

Answers

1. The Impossible Dream, in part because it was the team's first winning season since 1958.
2. Bob Gibson
3. Roger Maris
4. Red Sox pitcher Jim Lonborg, the American League Cy Young Award winner.
5. Julian Javier
6. Carl Yastrzemski
7. Mike Shannon
8. Roger Maris and Tim McCarver
9. Carl Yastrzemski, rookie Reggie Smith and Rico Petrocelli.
10. Bob Gibson

1975

1. True or false, Boston faced the three-time reigning World Series champion Oakland Athletics, who had a better regular-season record, in the American League Championship Series.

2. Who set the tone of the ALCS by allowing just one run on three hits in Game 1?

3. After falling into an early 3–0 hole, who led Boston's comeback with a two-run home run in Game 2?

4. Who earned his second save as Boston swept the series with a 5–3 victory in Game 3?

5. What were the Cincinnati Reds known as?

6. Who scored the first run in Game 1, when Boston put up six runs in the seventh inning?

7. Down 2–1 in the ninth inning of Game 2, who provided a two-out, game-tying single and subsequently scored the winning run for the Reds?

8. Although Game 3 is known for a controversial play in the 10th inning, when Boston thought interference should have been called, there were six home runs hit, three by each team. Who hit them? (Bonus: Which one was hit by a pinch-hitter?)

9. How many pitches did Luis Tiant throw in Game 4, while earning a 5–4 victory?

10. Who was hitless in the World Series before connecting for two home runs for the Reds in Game 5?

11. How many days after Game 5 was Game 6 played?

12. Who hit the three-run home run to tie Game 6 in the eighth inning?

13. During the famous 12th-inning home run by Carlton Fisk, why did NBC keep the camera on him as he waved at the ball to stay fair?

14. What was the first song Fenway Park organist John Kiley played following the home run?
15. Who singled in the winning run in the ninth inning of Game 7, to end what some call the best World Series ever played?

The iconic image: Carlton Fisk waves his walk-off home run fair. (Harry Cabluck)

Answers

1. True
2. Luis Tiant
3. Carl Yastrzemski
4. Dick Drago
5. The Big Red Machine
6. Starting pitcher Luis Tiant, who didn't bat during the regular season.
7. Dave Concepcion
8. Carlton Fisk, Bernie Carbo and Dwight Evans for Boston; Johnny Bench, Dave Concepción and Cesar Gerónimo for Cincinnati. Carbo was the pinch-hitter.
9. 163
10. Tony Perez
11. Five. After a travel day the series was delayed three days by rain.
12. Bernie Carbo, a former first-round pick of the Reds.
13. The cameraman had been distracted by a rat and wasn't able to follow the path of the ball until after it hit the foul pole.
14. Handel's "Hallelujah Chorus"
15. Joe Morgan

 **1986**

1. Long before Boston won the American League East, who hit the first pitch of the 1986 season for a home run?
2. Who threw a five-hitter for the California Angels in Game 1 of the American League Championship Series?
3. What left-hander got the win in Game 2 as Boston scored three runs in the seventh and eighth innings to pull away for a 9–2 victory?
4. Which two players hit home runs in the seventh inning to lead a 5–3 victory for the Angles in Game 3?
5. What relief pitcher got the win when the Angels pulled out a 4–3 victory in 11 innings?
6. Who hit a home run for the Red Sox when they were one strike away from elimination in Game 5?
7. Although the Angels scored two runs in the first inning, who got the win in Game 6?
8. Who helped lead an 8–1 victory with a three-run home run in Game 7?
9. What pitcher recorded his only postseason win for the Red Sox in Game 7?
10. Who committed the error that resulted in the only run in Game 1 of the World Series?
11. Who gave up eight hits and six runs (five earned) in five innings as Boston won 9–3 behind 18 hits in Game 2?
12. Who hit a leadoff home run to spark a four-run rally in the first inning that held up in Game 3?
13. Who threw seven scoreless innings to help the Mets tie the series with a 6–2 victory?
14. Who earned a complete-game victory in Game 5 to send the series back to New York with Boston leading 3–2?

15. Who hit what initially appeared to be the death blow to the Mets, a 10th-inning home run?

16. Down 5–3, who started the Mets' famous rally in the bottom of the 10th inning?

17. Who came into the game and threw a wild pitch that tied the score?

18. Who was the batter to hit the ground ball that went through Bill Buckner's legs?

19. Who were the winning pitchers of Game 6 and Game 7?

20. Who set a Major League record with 24 hits in 14 postseason games?

Answers

1. Dwight Evans off Jack Morris at Tigers Stadium.
2. Mike Witt
3. Bruce Hurst
4. Dick Schofield and Gary Pettis.
5. Doug Corbett
6. Dave Henderson
7. Oil Can Boyd
8. Jim Rice
9. Roger Clemens
10. Mets second baseman Tim Teufel.
11. Dwight Gooden
12. Lenny Dykstra
13. Ron Darling
14. Bruce Hurst. He was also the winning pitcher in Game 1.
15. Dave Henderson
16. Gary Carter, with Kevin Mitchell and Ray Knight following with base hits off Calvin Schiraldi to score Carter and bring the deficit to 5–4.
17. Bob Stanley on a 2–2 count. The Red Sox were one pitch away from winning the World Series when it occurred.
18. Mookie Wilson.
19. Rick Aguilera, who had given up the home run to Dave Henderson, and Roger McDowell.
20. Marty Barrett

 **1988**

1. Who, on the day Game 1 of the American League Championship Series was played, denied a report that he'd used steroids?
2. Who hit a home run in Game 1 to help lead the A's to a 2–1 victory?
3. What former Red Sox made an error that allowed a run to score in Game 2?
4. What reliever took the loss in Game 2?
5. Which five players hit home runs in Game 3, of which only one played for the Red Sox?
6. Who got the win in Game 4 as the Red Sox managed just four hits?
7. How many home runs did the A's hit in the series?
8. Who was named the MVP of the ALCS?
9. Why?
10. Who are the only other two pitchers in Major League playoff history to match that accomplishment?

Answers

1. José Canseco
2. José Canseco
3. Dave Henderson
4. Lee Smith
5. Mike Greenwell for the Red Sox, and Mark McGwire, Carney Lansford, Ron Hassey and Dave Henderson.
6. Dave Stewart
7. Seven, three by José Canseco
8. Dennis Eckersley
9. He recorded a save in all four games.
10. John Wetteland in the 1996 World Series and Greg Holland in the 2014 ALCS.

1990

1. True or false, of the four teams to make the postseason the Red Sox had the best record.
2. True or false, the Red Sox only scored one run in each game of the American League Championship Series.
3. How many runs did the bullpen give up in the ninth inning of Game 1?
4. Who hit the only home run for the Red Sox in the series in Game 1?
5. What pitcher, who would soon be announced as the Cy Young Award winner, got the win in Game 2?
6. Who tried to steal home during Game 3?
7. Who was ejected for arguing balls and strikes during Game 4?
8. Who was also ejected after the subsequent argument?
9. Who was named the series MVP?
10. Which number was bigger for Boston in the series, runs scored or errors made?

 **1995**

1. True or false, the season was shortened to 144 games in an experiment to see if it might improve the quality of play.

2. True or false, 1995 was the first season with expanded playoffs and the inclusion of a wild-card team.

3. Why did the Red Sox play the 100-win Cleveland Indians in a Division Series when the Seattle Mariners had the worst record of the four American League playoffs teams?

4. How long had it been since Cleveland played a postseason game?

5. Who hit a game-winning home run with two outs in the 13th inning of Game 1?

6. What starting pitcher earned the win and helped lead a 4–0 shutout in Game 2?

7. Who hit a two-run home run to spark the Indians' offense in Game 3?

8. What pitcher took the loss?

9. True or false, the Red Sox actually outhit the Indians in the series.

10. True or false, the Indians went on to win the World Series.

Answers

1. False, it was shortened due to a players' strike.
2. True
3. Because the New York Yankees beat out the Red Sox in the East and two teams from the same division couldn't play in the first round of the playoffs.
4. Since 1954
5. Tony Pena
6. Orel Hershiser
7. Jim Thome
8. Tim Wakefield
9. False. The Red Sox were outscored 17–6, but only outhit 25–21.
10. False. The Braves beat the Indians in the World Series 4–2.

1998

1. Although Boston finished the regular season 92–70, and second in the American League East, how many games did it finish behind the New York Yankees?

2. Who hit a three-run home run in the first inning of Game 1 for Boston?

3. Who slugged a three-run home run later in the game?

4. Who got the win?

5. The win snapped how long of a postseason losing streak for the Red Sox?

6. Who was ejected after Boston took a 2–0 lead in the first inning of Game 2?

7. Who led the Indians' comeback with a sacrifice fly and a three-run home run?

8. What Red Sox pitcher took the loss in Game 3?

9. Who hit a two-run home run to bring Boston within one run in the bottom of the ninth?

10. Who took the loss in Game 4 by giving up two runs in the eighth inning as the Indians clinched the series?

Answers

1. 22
2. Mo Vaughn, who had another home run and a two-run double to lead the 11–3 victory
3. Nomar Garciaparra
4. Pedro Martinez
5. 13 games.
6. Cleveland manager Mike Hargrove and starter Dwight Gooden were both ejected from the game.
7. David Justice
8. Bret Saberhagen
9. Nomar Garciaparra
10. Tom Gordon

 **1999**

1. Although Boston finished the regular season 94–68, and again second in the American League East, how many games did it finish behind the New York Yankees?

2. Who had to leave in the fifth inning of Game 1 of the American League Division Series with 2–0 lead?

3. Who hit a grand slam in Game 2 to help give the Indians a 2–0 lead?

4. Who had a home run and a two-run double to help lead Boston's 9–3 victory in Game 3?

5. How many runs did the Red Sox score in Game 4?

6. After the two teams combined to score 15 runs during the first three innings, who came out of the bullpen and threw six hitless innings, striking out eight and walking three?

7. Who was fired at the end of the series?

8. In the American League Championship Series, which rival did the Red Sox meet in the postseason for the first time?

9. Who hit a leadoff home run in the 10th inning to win Game 1?

10. Who got the win in Game 1 and the save in Game 2?

11. Who did the Red Sox pound in Game 3 en route to a 13–1 victory?

12. Who struck out 12 Yankees in seven scoreless innings and allowed just two hits to get the win, and finished the playoffs with a streak of 17 scoreless innings?

13. Who was Chuck Knoblauch trying to tag out during "The Phantom Tag" in the eighth inning of Game 4?

14. Who hit a grand slam in the ninth inning of Game 4?

15. Who hit a two-run home run in the first inning to help pace a 6–1 series-ending victory in Game 5?

Answers

1. 4
2. Pedro Martinez, the Cy Young Award winner, due to an injury. Cleveland came back and won, 3–2.
3. Jim Thome
4. John Valentin
5. 23, while Cleveland scored seven, to tie up the best-of-five series.
6. Pedro Martinez, and the Red Sox won 12–8
7. Indians manager Mike Hargrove
8. The New York Yankees.
9. Bernie Williams off Rod Beck.
10. Mariano Rivera
11. Roger Clemens
12. Pedro Martinez
13. José Offerman
14. Ricky Ledée
15. Derek Jeter

2003

1. Coming into the series how many consecutive playoff games had the A's defeated the Red Sox?
2. Who laid down a two-out bunt single in the 14th inning to bring in the winning run during Game 1 of the American League Division Series?
3. Who had a two-run throwing error as part of a five-run inning as Oakland won Game 2, 5–1, and was just one win away from the American League Championship Series?
4. Who had a two-run walk-off home run in the 11th inning of Game 3 as Boston finally snapped its playoff losing streak to Oakland?
5. Who had a game-winning two-RBI double in the eighth inning for Boston in Game 4?
6. Who hit a three-run home run in Game 5 to complete Boston's comeback in the series?
7. What pitcher foiled the host Yankees in Game 1 of the American League Championship Series?
8. Who answered with a similar performance for the Yankees in Game 2?
9. With tempers flaring and a brawl breaking out during Game 3, who charged Pedro Martinez only to get thrown to the ground after the pitcher sidestepped him?
10. Who hit a home run to pace Boston, and who beat a potential double-play ground ball with the bases loaded as the winning run scored in the seventh inning?
11. Which two Yankees pitchers combined to lead a 4–2 victory in Game 5?
12. Who was the winning pitcher in Game 6 thanks to Boston rallying for three runs in the seventh inning?
13. What controversial move did Boston manager Grady Little make in the eighth inning of Game 7?

14. How many home runs did the Red Sox hit in the series?
15. How many games did the Yankees and Red Sox play in 2003?

Answers

1. Eight, which was then tied for the most consecutive playoff wins against one team, a record set by the New York Yankees against the Chicago Cubs with World Series sweeps in 1932 and 1938.
2. Catcher Ramón Hernández, to score Eric Chávez from third base.
3. Todd Walker
4. Trot Nixon
5. David Ortiz
6. Manny Ramirez
7. Tim Wakefield as Boston won 5–2.
8. Andy Pettitte
9. Yankees bench coach Don Zimmer, who was 72 at the time. The Yankees won 4–3, with Roger Clemens getting the win.
10. Todd Walker and Jason Varitek.
11. David Wells and Mariano Rivera.
12. Alan Embree
13. He left Pedro Martinez in the game after throwing 100 pitches. The Yankees rallied for three runs to tie the the game, and then won in the 11th on Aaron Boone's game-winning home run. Little's contract was not renewed during the offseason and he was replaced by Terry Francona.
14. 12, an ALCS record.
15. 26 times, which set a Major League record for a single season.

2004

1. Although the Red Sox were the American League wild-card team again, how close did they come to reaching 100 wins during the regular season?

2. Who got the win in Game 1 of the American League Division Series, but injured his ankle?

3. After the Anaheim Angels took their only lead of the series in Game 2, who answered with a two-out, two-run home run in the sixth inning?

4. Who hit a grand slam to help erase a 6–1 deficit in Game 3?

5. Whose walk-off home run in the 10th inning ended the series?

6. Who retired the first 19 Red Sox batters he faced as the Yankees jumped out to an 8–0 lead in Game 1 of the American League Championship Series?

7. Who got the win against Pedro Martinez in Game 2?

8. How many hits did the Yankees crank out in Game 3?

9. With Boston just three outs away from elimination, who singled, who stole second base, and who knocked in the tying run off closer Mariano Rivera?

10. Who hit a walk-off home run in the 12th inning for the Red Sox?

11. With two outs in the 14th inning of Game 5, on what pitch of his at-bat did David Ortiz single in the winning run?

12. Why was Curt Schilling's performance in Game 6 so memorable?

13. After the game, what did Schilling's T-shirt read during his postgame press conference?

14. What movie did the Red Sox watch before Game 7?

15. Who hit two home runs including a grand slam, and was responsible for bringing in six runs during the 10–3 victory in Game 7?

16. True or false, the Red Sox were the first team in Major League history to lose the first three games and win the next four to win a seven-game series.

17. Who hit a three-run home run in his first World Series at-bat in Game 1?

18. Who hit a two-run home run off the right field foul pole at Fenway Park to give the Red Sox a two-run lead in the eighth inning?

19. Who threw six scoreless innings to get the win in Game 2?

20. Who made three errors during Game 2 to tie a World Series record?

21. In 22 at-bats during the first two games, how many hits had Cardinals batters Scott Rolen, Jim Edmonds and Reggie Sanders combined for?

22. Who, after loading the bases and having a runner thrown out at the plate, threw eight scoreless innings, allowing just three hits and retired the last 14 batters faced?

23. Who led off Game 4 with a home run for the Red Sox?

24. Who became the first pitcher to ever win three series clinching games in a single postseason?

25. Who said after the Red Sox won their first World Series in 86 years: "I don't believe in curses, I believe you make your own destination."

Pedro Martinez celebrates after the Red Sox' historic 2004 ALCS comeback ended with a 10–3 defeat of the Yankees in Game 7. (Charles Krupa)

Answers

1. Two wins, Boston finished 98–64, while the New York Yankees were 101–61. The St. Louis Cardinals had the best record in baseball at 105–57.
2. Curt Schilling. Specifically, he sustained a torn tendon sheath in his right ankle.
3. Jason Varitek
4. Vladimir Guerrero for the Angels
5. David Ortiz
6. Mike Mussina. Boston did cut the deficit to 8–7, but ended up losing 10–7.
7. Jon Lieber
8. 22 as they crushed the Red Sox 19–8 to take a 3–0 lead in the series. Hideki Matsui had five hits and five RBIs, tying LCS records, and both he and Alex Rodriguez tied the postseason record for runs scored with five.
9. Kevin Millar had the leadoff hit, pinch-runner Dave Roberts stole second after numerous throws to first, and Bill Mueller singled in the run.
10. David Ortiz, making him the first player with two walk-off home runs in the same postseason.
11. The 10th, for a 5–4 victory.
12. After having an unprecedented procedure by Red Sox team doctors to help stabilize the tendon in his ankle, Schilling threw seven strong innings while the blood on his sock was visible. After being ineffective in Game 1, he got the win as Boston tied up the series with a 4–2 victory.
13. "Why Not Us?" It was the team slogan that year.
14. *Miracle*, the movie about the 1980 U.S. men's gold-medal hockey team.
15. Johnny Damon
16. True
17. David Ortiz. He finished with four RBIs, tying a franchise World Series record, as Boston went on to win 11–9. It was the highest scoring opening game in World Series history.
18. Mark Bellhorn
19. Curt Schilling, who had had four stitches put into his injured ankle the day before. One was removed the day of the game. With the win, Schilling became only the fifth pitcher to ever win a World Series game with a team from both leagues.
20. Bill Mueller
21. One
22. Pedro Martinez
23. Johnny Damon
24. Derek Lowe, as Boston won Game 7, 3–0. The Cardinals managed just four hits.
25. Series MVP Manny Ramirez, who hit .412 (7-for-17).

2005

1. Why were the Red Sox designated the wild-card team for the playoffs after tying for the American League East title?

2. Who entered the postseason with a hot bat, having been named the American League's Player of the Month for September and led the league in RBIs?

3. What happened during the first at-bat against Boston starter Matt Clement in Game 1 of the Division Series?

4. The 14–2 victory was the Chicago White Sox' first postseason win since what year?

5. Whose error in the fifth inning helped lead to three unearned runs in Game 2?

6. What pitcher took the loss?

7. Who hit two home runs for the Red Sox in Game 3?

8. Who took the loss?

9. True or false, the Red Sox actually outhit the White Sox in the series.

10. It was the first postseason series win for the White Sox since what year?

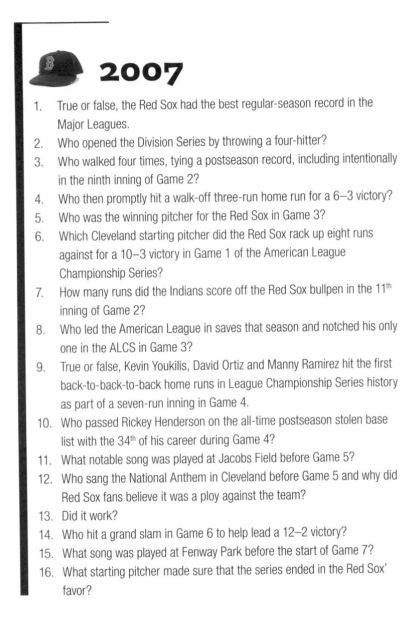

2007

1. True or false, the Red Sox had the best regular-season record in the Major Leagues.

2. Who opened the Division Series by throwing a four-hitter?

3. Who walked four times, tying a postseason record, including intentionally in the ninth inning of Game 2?

4. Who then promptly hit a walk-off three-run home run for a 6–3 victory?

5. Who was the winning pitcher for the Red Sox in Game 3?

6. Which Cleveland starting pitcher did the Red Sox rack up eight runs against for a 10–3 victory in Game 1 of the American League Championship Series?

7. How many runs did the Indians score off the Red Sox bullpen in the 11th inning of Game 2?

8. Who led the American League in saves that season and notched his only one in the ALCS in Game 3?

9. True or false, Kevin Youkilis, David Ortiz and Manny Ramirez hit the first back-to-back-to-back home runs in League Championship Series history as part of a seven-run inning in Game 4.

10. Who passed Rickey Henderson on the all-time postseason stolen base list with the 34th of his career during Game 4?

11. What notable song was played at Jacobs Field before Game 5?

12. Who sang the National Anthem in Cleveland before Game 5 and why did Red Sox fans believe it was a ploy against the team?

13. Did it work?

14. Who hit a grand slam in Game 6 to help lead a 12–2 victory?

15. What song was played at Fenway Park before the start of Game 7?

16. What starting pitcher made sure that the series ended in the Red Sox' favor?

17. Which National League team was undefeated in the postseason and had won 21 of its last 22 regular-season games en route to the World Series?
18. Who hit a leadoff home run in Game 1?
19. Who's the only other player to do that in World Series history?
20. How many bases-loaded walks did the Red Sox draw during Game 1?
21. What did Jonathan Papelbon do for the first time in his career during Game 2?
22. What did starting pitcher Daisuke Matsuzaka do for the first time in the Major Leagues during Game 3?
23. Who made the final out of the World Series?
24. How many doubles did the Red Sox hit to set a World Series record?
25. Who was named World Series MVP?

Answers

1. True. They were tied with the Cleveland Indians for the best record, 96–66. The Red Sox received home-field advantage by virtue of winning the season series, 5–2.
2. The only 20-game winner in the majors that year, Josh Beckett, for a 4–0 victory.
3. David Ortiz
4. Manny Ramirez
5. Curt Schilling
6. CC Sabathia
7. Seven
8. Joe Borowski
9. False. The home runs and record are true, however they were part of a three-run sixth inning after Cleveland scored seven runs in the fifth en route to a 7–3 victory and 3–1 lead in the series.
10. Kenny Lofton
11. The All-American Rejects hit song "It Ends Tonight"
12. Danielle Peck, who had dated Game 5 starter Josh Beckett the previous summer.
13. Nope. Cleveland's only run came on a double-play groundout. He pitched eight innings and struck out 11 as the Red Sox won 7–1.
14. J.D. Drew
15. "It Ends Tonight"
16. Rookie Daisuke Matsuzaka as the Red Sox won 11–2.
17. The Colorado Rockies, making it the Rox vs. Sox Series.
18. Rookie Dustin Pedroia
19. Baltimore's Don Buford in 1969.
20. Three as the Red Sox easily won, 13–1.
21. Picked off a base runner, Matt Holliday, who had four of Colorado's five hits in the game. He was picked off in the eighth inning as Boston won 2–1.
22. Get a base hit. He helped his cause with a bases-loaded two-RBI single as Boston went on to win 10–5. Matsuzaka also became the first Japanese pitcher to start and win a World Series game.
23. Pinch hitter Seth Smith. He struck out as Jonathan Papelbon earned his third save.
24. 18
25. Mike Lowell. He hit .400 (6-for-15), with three doubles, a home run and six RBIs.

2008

1. Which playoff team had the best regular-season record in the Major Leagues?

2. What late-season acquisition hit a two-run home run to give Boston the lead in Game 1 of its American League Division Series?

3. Who hit a three-run home run in the first frame, and who hit a two-run shot in the final frame, to lead a 7–5 victory in Game 2?

4. What future Red Sox hit two home runs and scored the winning run on an error in the 12th inning in Game 3?

5. Before that loss, in how many consecutive postseason games had the Red Sox defeated the Angels to set a Major League record?

6. Who had a walk-off single in the ninth inning of Game 4 to end the series?

7. What starting pitcher didn't give up a hit in Game 1 of the American League Championship Series until Carl Crawford singled in the seventh inning?

8. Who hit two of the seven home runs in Game 2, only to see his team lose on a sacrifice fly in the 11th inning?

9. Which New England product hit a three-run home run over the Green Monster for Tampa Bay in Game 3?

10. What future Red Sox went 5-for-5 with two stolen bases to help lead a 13–4 victory in Game 4?

11. With Boston on the brink of elimination and trailing 7–0 in Game 5, what player hit a three-run home run in the seventh to help spark a comeback?

12. Who subsequently hit a two-run home run in the eighth and singled in the game-winning run in the ninth?

13. Who picked a really good time to have his first hit in the series by hitting a home run in the sixth inning of Game 6?

14. After Game 6 what was manager Terry Francona's record in elimination games with the Red Sox?

15. What starting pitcher threw a gem in Game 7 to be named the series MVP, and what future Cy Young winner threw the ninth to get the save?

Answers

1. Los Angeles Angels of Anaheim, who were 100–62. Boston was 95–67, two games behind Tampa Bay in the American League East.
2. Jason Bay
3. Jason Bay had the first-inning home run, and J.D. Drew hit the ninth-inning home run for the Red Sox.
4. Mike Napoli
5. 11, dating back to 1986.
6. Jed Lowrie
7. Daisuke Matsuzaka
8. Dustin Pedroia
9. Rocco Baldelli, as the Devil Rays won 7–1.
10. Carl Crawford
11. David Ortiz, ending a drought of 61 postseason at-bats without a home run.
12. J.D. Drew
13. Jason Varitek, as Boston won 4–2 to force Game 7.
14. 9–1
15. Matt Garza and David Price.

2009

1. True or false, the Red Sox had the worst record of the American League playoff teams, but would have had the best record in the National League.
2. Who threw the first postseason shutout in Angels history in Game 1 of the Division Series?
3. In Game 2 who took the first loss in nine postseason starts for the Red Sox?
4. Who ended up taking the loss as Boston blew a 5–1 lead in Game 3?
5. Who knocked in the series-clinching run with a bases-loaded single in the ninth inning?

Answers

1. False, but it was pretty close. Boston finished 95–67, which matched the Los Angeles Dodgers in the National League, but the Minnesota Twins squeaked into the playoffs by winning the American League Central at 87–76.
2. John Lackey as Los Angeles won 5–0.
3. Josh Beckett as the Angels won 4–1.
4. Jonathan Papelbon
5. Vladimir Guerrero

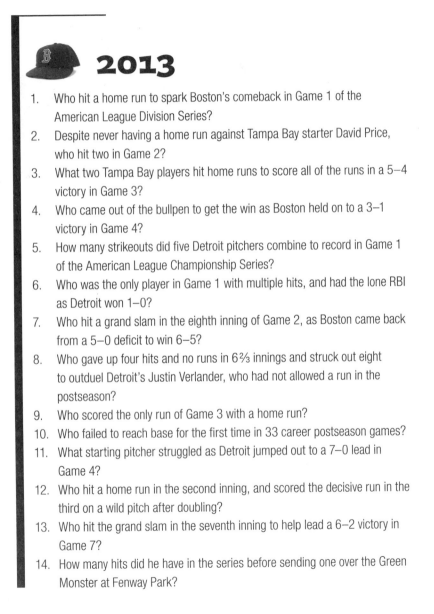

2013

1. Who hit a home run to spark Boston's comeback in Game 1 of the American League Division Series?

2. Despite never having a home run against Tampa Bay starter David Price, who hit two in Game 2?

3. What two Tampa Bay players hit home runs to score all of the runs in a 5–4 victory in Game 3?

4. Who came out of the bullpen to get the win as Boston held on to a 3–1 victory in Game 4?

5. How many strikeouts did five Detroit pitchers combine to record in Game 1 of the American League Championship Series?

6. Who was the only player in Game 1 with multiple hits, and had the lone RBI as Detroit won 1–0?

7. Who hit a grand slam in the eighth inning of Game 2, as Boston came back from a 5–0 deficit to win 6–5?

8. Who gave up four hits and no runs in 6⅔ innings and struck out eight to outduel Detroit's Justin Verlander, who had not allowed a run in the postseason?

9. Who scored the only run of Game 3 with a home run?

10. Who failed to reach base for the first time in 33 career postseason games?

11. What starting pitcher struggled as Detroit jumped out to a 7–0 lead in Game 4?

12. Who hit a home run in the second inning, and scored the decisive run in the third on a wild pitch after doubling?

13. Who hit the grand slam in the seventh inning to help lead a 6–2 victory in Game 7?

14. How many hits did he have in the series before sending one over the Green Monster at Fenway Park?

Jonny Gomes, Jacoby Ellsbury, and Dustin Pedroia celebrate a three-run double by Mike Napoli during the first inning of Game 1 of the 2013 World Series. (Charlie Riedel)

15. Who was named the ALCS MVP?

16. Who was accused of using a foreign substance on his glove during Game 1 of the World Series, but claimed that it was just rosin (which is legal)?

17. Who hit a two-run home run for Boston's only runs of Game 2?

18. Who was called for obstruction in the bottom of the ninth inning, resulting the Cardinals' game-winning run in Game 3?

19. Who hit a three-run home run in the sixth inning that ended up being the difference in Game 4?

20. Game 4 was the first postseason game in baseball history to end how?

21. Who joined Babe Ruth as the only Red Sox left-handers to win three World Series games with a 3–1 victory in Game 5?

22. With a 6–1 victory in Game 6, what did the Red Sox do at Fenway Park for the first time since 1918?

23. Who took the loss after being previously unbeaten in the playoffs?

24. Who was walked by the Cardinals four times, and scored twice?

25. Who opened the scoring in Game 6 with a three-run double in the third inning and had four RBIs?

Answers

1. No one. Boston had 14 hits en route to a 12–2 victory over Tampa Bay, but had no home runs at Fenway Park.
2. David Ortiz
3. Evan Longoria and José Lobatón.
4. Craig Breslow
5. 17. They also had a no-hitter going through 8⅓ innings.
6. Jhonny Peralta
7. David Ortiz
8. John Lackey
9. Mike Napoli
10. Miguel Cabrera
11. Jake Peavy, as the Tigers won 7–3 and evened the series at 2–2.
12. Mike Napoli
13. Shane Victorino
14. He previously was 2-for-23 in the series.
15. Closer Koji Uehara, who had three saves.
16. Jon Lester, who earned the win as the Red Sox cruised to an 8–1 victory.
17. David Ortiz
18. Will Middlebrooks. Third-base umpire Jim Joyce made the call, and home-plate umpire Dana DeMuth upheld it, ruling that base runner Allen Craig (who had knocked down Middlebrooks while sliding into third, resulting in the ball caroming into foul territory following a play at the plate) would have scored anyway.
19. Jonny Gomes
20. With a pickoff. Boston closer Koji Uehara picked off pinch-runner Kolten Wong with Carlos Beltran at the plate. The Red Sox won 4–2.
21. Jon Lester
22. Win the World Series.
23. Michael Wacha
24. Series MVP David Ortiz
25. Shane Victorino

Fourteen

The Babe

If you're a die-hard Red Sox fan you might want to skip this part.

We understand, but would be remiss if Babe Ruth wasn't included in this book in some way. Granted he went on to hammer the Red Sox for the rest of his career, and there's that whole "Curse of the Bambino" thing, but he also had some amazing years with the Red Sox before owner Harry Frazee traded him.

According to the *Boston Globe* on January 6, 1920, here's what Frazee said when announcing the move at Red Sox headquarters in the Carney Building, while declining to give the details of the deal:

The price was something enormous, but I do not care to name the figures. It was an amount the club could not afford to refuse.

I should have preferred to have taken players in exchange for Ruth, but no club could have given me the equivalent in men without wrecking itself, and so the deal had to be made on a cash basis.

No other club could afford to give the amount the Yankees have paid for him, and I do not mind saying I think they are taking a gamble.

With this money the Boston club can now go into the market and buy other players and have a stronger and better team in all respects than we would have if Ruth had remained with us.

I do not wish to detract one iota from Ruth's ability as a ball player nor from his value as an attraction, but there is no getting away from the fact that despite his 29 home runs, the Red Sox finished sixth in the race last season.

What the Boston fans want, I take it, and what I want because they want it, is a winning team, rather than a one-man team which finishes in sixth place.

From 1914–19 Ruth had won three World Series with the Red Sox and made the conversion from outstanding pitcher to slugger.

During his 15 years with New York, he helped the Yankees win seven American League championships and four World Series titles.

In the 84 years following the deal, the Yankees played in 39 World Series, winning 26, while the Red Sox played in only four and lost each in seven games.

The Babe

1. Where was George Herman Ruth, Jr. born on February 6, 1895?
2. Where did he attend school?
3. With which minor-league team did he sign, which eventually sold his rights to the Boston Red Sox?
4. Which teammates were also sold to the Red Sox?
5. How old was Ruth when he made his Major League debut?
6. True or false, Ruth lost his first game pitching in the majors.
7. What did Babe Ruth do at the plate in his first at-bat on July 11, 1914?
8. What was his record during his first season in the pitching rotation in 1915?
9. In what two statistical categories did Ruth lead all American League pitchers in 1916?

10. True or false, one of those still stands as a Major League record for left-handed pitchers.
11. True or false, Ruth is the youngest pitcher in Red Sox history to win a postseason game.
12. True or false, Ruth threw a no-hitter in 1917.
13. Who urged manager Ed Barrow to start letting Ruth hit more and not just pitch?
14. In 1918, who did Ruth tie for the Major League lead in home runs?
15. How many consecutive scoreless innings did Ruth pitch in the World Series?
16. Who eventually broke that World Series record?
17. What did Babe Ruth do for the first time on May 20, 1919?
18. How many home runs did he hit during his final season with the Red Sox, 1919?
19. In which of the following statistical categories did he also lead the Major Leagues in 1919: on-base percentage, RBIs, runs, slugging percentage and/or total bases?
20. Out of the 714 home runs Babe Ruth hit, how many were for the Red Sox?
21. Who also joined the Yankees after the 1920 season?
22. True or false, Ruth never pitched for the Yankees.
23. Ruth is one of eight pitchers in Major League history to never have a losing record over a career spanning at least 10 years. Name the other seven.
24. Who is the only player in Major League history to have more walk-off home runs than Ruth's 12?
25. Why do some fans believe that the "Curse of the Bambino" was specifically snapped when a foul ball hit a boy in the stands on August 31, 2004?

Answers

1. Baltimore, Maryland
2. St. Mary's Industrial School for Boys
3. The Baltimore Orioles
4. Pitchers Ernie Shore and Ben Egan. After two weeks with Boston, Egan was traded to Cleveland.
5. 19
6. False, he won as Boston defeated the Cleveland Naps, 4–3.
7. He struck out
8. 18–8 with a 2.44 ERA
9. ERA (1.75) and shutouts (nine). Ruth posted a record of 23–12.
10. True. Ron Guidry tied the nine shutouts in 1978.
11. True. He was 21 years, 246 days old when he won Game 2 of the 1916 World Series.
12. False, but in 1991 Major League Baseball's Committee on Statistical Accuracy gave him credit for a combined no-hitter at Washington on June 23, 1917. Ruth started, but when the home plate umpire called the first four pitches as balls, Ruth threw a punch at him. Ruth was ejected and later suspended for ten days. Ernie Shore took his place and retired the next 26 batters.
13. Harry Hooper. Barrow had been the president of the International League, but was inexperienced as a manager.
14. Tillie Walker of the Philadelphia Athletics. They both hit 11 home runs.
15. 29 ⅔, which at the time was a record.
16. Whitey Ford in 1961.
17. He hit his first grand slam during a 6–4 victory against the St. Louis Browns.
18. 29, which set a Major League record.
19. All of them.
20. 49
21. Ed Barrow as general manager. He made a number of deals with the Red Sox that helped keep Frazee financially afloat.
22. False, but he only pitched five times over the rest of his career.
23. Spud Chandler, Dizzy Dean, Dave Foutz, Joe McGinnity, Deacon Phillippe, Jay Powell and Urban Shocker.
24. Jim Thome
25. The foul ball hit by Manny Ramirez flew into Section 9, Box AA and struck 16-year-old Lee Gavin in the face, knocking two of his teeth out. Gavin lived on the Sudbury farm owned by Ruth. That same day, the Yankees suffered their worst loss in team history, 22–0 to the Cleveland Indians.

Fifteen

Miscellaneous

From the stadiums to World Series and the Hall of Famers, just about every aspect of the Red Sox has been covered, right?

Hardly.

This section will test your knowledge of everything else in a very random way, from the odd moments to the unusual statistics that just don't quite fit in anywhere else.

 # Miscellaneous

1. When the Red Sox Hall of Fame was created in 1995, 14 people were automatically inducted due to already being in the National Baseball Hall of Fame and Museum in Cooperstown, N.Y. Name them. (Hint: The key word is "people".)
2. There were six people in the initial induction class for the Red Sox Hall of Fame who were not in the National Baseball Hall of Fame. Name them.
3. What front-office executive with an especially famous name for New England was inducted into the Red Sox Hall of Fame in 2008?
4. What groundskeeper was inducted into the Red Sox Hall of Fame in 2012?
5. In whose honor is the press box at Fenway Park named?

6. Clay Buchholz is one of three pitchers since 1900 to throw a no-hitter in either his first or second Major League start. Who were the first two?

7. Which two players in Red Sox history have made an unassisted triple play?

8. Who is the only man to play on four Red Sox World Championship teams?

9. Who is the only other player who was on four Red Sox title teams?

10. Who are the only two Red Sox players who successfully pulled off the hidden ball play more than once?

11. On July 17, 1990, the Red Sox became the first team in Major League history to hit into two triple plays in one game. Who was the opponent?

12. What kept Ted Williams from winning the 1955 batting title?

13. Who holds the Red Sox record for consecutive home runs in the shortest time in terms of innings, three home runs in two innings?

14. In 1986 the Yankees finished second to the Red Sox in the standings. When was the last time that occurred?

15. A little over two months after Babe Ruth hit his first career home run, he hit a memorable shot out of Sportsman's Park on July 21, 1915. Where did it end up?

16. What rookie pitcher had more starts than Roger Clemens in 2007?

17. On the all-time Red Sox roster who is first and last among the coaches?

18. Roger Clemens is one of three pitchers in Major League history with 20-win seasons in three separate decades. Who are the other two?

19. Since 1814, who is the only Red Sox player to finish a season with an on-base streak of at least 35 games?

20. Why did Babe Ruth only tie for the American League lead in home runs with 11 and not win it outright in 1918?

21. Who was the first pitcher with three 20-win seasons with three different teams?

22. Who served up the pitch that Jimmie Foxx hit for home run No. 500?

23. Between hits, home runs, and RBIs, in which is David Ortiz the all-time leader as a designated hitter?

24. Since the designated hitter rule was adopted, three Red Sox pitchers have

recorded a hit in non-interleague games. Name them.

25. On June 8, 1950, the Boston Red Sox won 29–4 and set new American League single-game records for runs scored during a game, extra base hits, and total bases. Name the opponent.

26. In that game, who set a Major League record as becoming the only batter to have ever batted eight times in eight innings?

27. Since 1972 only two Red Sox have had 40-plus game-tying or go-ahead RBIs but didn't lead the team in that statistic. Name them.

28. When Pedro Martinez was the 2000 American League ERA champion, who was second?

29. Who as a rookie threw out a Major League-best 51.7 percent of attempted base stealers (15 of 29), the best rate in Red Sox history?

30. True or false, the Red Sox are the only team to go from last place to a World Series back to last place over three consecutive seasons.

31. True or false, the Red Sox have won a tie-breaker game to get into the American League playoffs.

32. Name the four professional football teams that called Fenway Park home.

33. Which prominent baseball writer joined the Red Sox as a Senior Baseball Operations Advisor in November 2002?

34. In 2013 Xander Bogaerts became the second-youngest player ever to start each World Series game for the winning side. Who was the youngest?

35. Heading into the 2016 season who was the last player to play in every Red Sox game of a season?

36. Who was the first player in Red Sox history to have a 20/20 season, 20 home runs and 20 stolen bases?

37. Which future Red Sox was named *USA Today's* High School Player of the Year in 2007?

38. What player set the record for most hits in a single postseason before he joined the Red Sox?

39. Heading into the 2016 season, who has the best career batting average in the World Series (minimum 50 at-bats)?

40. What's the lowest ERA posted by a Red Sox pitcher since 1915 (minimum 40 innings pitched)?

41. In baseball statistics, walks plus hits per inning pitched (WHIP) is considered a Sabermetric measurement of the number of base-runners a pitcher has allowed per inning pitched. Who had the best single-season WHIP in Red Sox history? (Hint: Dennis Eckersley had the second and third best.)

42. Who is the only Red Sox player to have won the Heart and Hustle Award, which is given annually by the Major League Baseball Players Alumni Association?

43. Which four Red Sox have served as the American League honorary captain of the All-Star Game?

44. Other than Ted Williams, who did it twice, who is the only player in Red Sox history to knock in 40 runs in a month?

45. Who is the only pitcher in Red Sox history to take the loss in a game he hit a grand slam?

46. Of all the Red Sox' team batting leaders, who had the lowest batting average?

47. On July 28, 1943, Babe Ruth and Ted Williams had a home run hitting contest at Yankee Stadium as part of a charity day for the Red Cross and the benefit raised more than $30,000. Who won?

48. What was the Boudreau Shift?

49. What happened when the Red Sox saw the maneuver again on September 13, 1946?

50. During his Hall of Fame induction speech, who did Ted Williams plead for the inclusion of into the Baseball Hall of Fame?

Answers

1. Eddie Collins (front office), Jimmy Collins, Joe Cronin, Bobby Doerr, Jimmie Foxx, Curt Gowdy (broadcaster), Lefty Grove, Harry Hooper, Rick Ferrell, Herb Pennock, Red Ruffing, Babe Ruth, Tris Speaker, Ted Williams, Carl Yastrzemski, Tom Yawkey (longtime owner), Cy Young.
2. The rest of the Class of 1995 was Tony Conigliaro, Dom DiMaggio, Frank Malzone, Johnny Pesky, Smoky Joe Wood and Jean R. Yawkey (owner).
3. Edward Kennedy Sr., who worked for the team for 43 years (1948–191).
4. Joe Mooney
5. Richard Louis Bresciani, who worked for the team for 42 years and was known as "Bresh."
6. Bobo Holloman for the St. Louis Browns against the Philadelphia Athletics on May 6, 1953 and Wilson Alvarez for the Chicago White Sox against the Baltimore Orioles on August 11, 1991.
7. George Burns in 1923 and John Valentin in 1994.
8. Harry Hooper (1912, 1915, 1916 & 1918).
9. Heinie Wagner was part of those same four Red Sox championship teams.
10. Marty Barrett and Johnny Pesky both pulled it off three times.
11. The Minnesota Twins.
12. Due to being walked 71 times Williams did not have enough at-bats to win the batting champion title. A rule change occurred by the following season changing the batting title criteria to plate appearances versus times at-bat. Williams had a .356 average, but Al Kaline was the batting champion at .340.
13. Nomar Garciaparra on July 23, 2002.
14. 1904
15. After clearing the right field stands it crossed Grand Avenue and broke the window of a car dealer.
16. Al Nipper
17. Luis Alicea (2007–08) and Don Zimmer (1974–76, 1992)
18. Bob Feller and Warren Spahn.
19. Mo Vaughn in 1998.
20. At the time games were "complete" when the winning run crossed the plate during the ninth inning. On July 8 he hit a home run in the ninth inning, but due to the rule was only credited with a triple and RBI.
21. Carl Mays. He went 22–9 with the Boston Red Sox in 1917, 26–22 with the New York Yankees in 1920, and 20–9 with the Cincinnati Reds in 1924.
22. George Caster of the Philadelphia Athletics on September 24, 1940.
23. All of them
24. Pete Schourek, Roger Clemens and Tim Lollar.
25. The St. Louis Browns
26. Leadoff batter Clyde Vollmer
27. Jim Rice in 1979 (41), and Manny Ramirez in 2004 (41).
28. Roger Clemens. Martinez had a 1.74 ERA while Clemens was second at 3.70.
29. Christian Vazquez in 2014.
30. True.

31. False, the Red Sox have played in two and lost them both. In 1948 they lost 8–3 to Cleveland to decide the pennant, and in 1978 the New York Yankees won 5–4 in the famous "#$@$!*% Bucky Dent" game. Both games were played at Fenway Park.
32. The Boston Patriots, Boston Shamrocks, Boston Redskins and Boston Yanks all played professional football games at Fenway Park.
33. Bill James
34. Miguel Cabrera with the Florida Marlins.
35. Right fielder Dwight Evans in 1984.
36. Jackie Jensen in 1954. He was also the second player to do so in 1959.
37. Rick Porcello
38. Pablo Sandoval with 26 for the San Francisco Giants in 2014.
39. David Ortiz with a .455 batting average.
40. 0.92 by Jonathan Papelbon in 2006.
41. Koji Uehara in 2013 with a 0.57 WHIP.
42. Dustin Pedroia in 2013.
43. Joe Cronin (1983), Bobby Doerr (1988), Carlton Fisk (1999), and Carl Yastrzemski (1989).
44. Clyde Vollmer with 40 in July 1951, in 29 games. Williams has the team record with 41 in May 1942 (28 games), and he had 40 RBIs in June 1950 (29 games).
45. Lefty Grove on July 27, 1935. The Red Sox lost 7–6 at the Philadelphia Athletics.
46. Tom Brunansky, who hit .266 in 1992.
47. Ted Williams (although in fairness to Babe Ruth he did have a bad knee at the time).
48. It was a defensive maneuver the Cleveland Indians did against Ted Williams with six players moving to the right side of second base and the left fielder being repositioned at shortstop, making him the only player left of second base. The Indians debuted it on July 14, 1946, and Williams promptly hit a double down the right field line. "We had to do something" player/manager Lou Boudreau of the Cleveland Indians said. Incidentally, he joined the Red Sox in 1952.
49. Ted Williams hit the ball to left field for the only inside-the-park home run of his career and gave Boston a 1–0 victory that clinched the American League pennant. He later called it the hardest home run of his career because he had to run.
50. Negro League players including Satchel Paige and Josh Gibson. On June 10, 1971, the Hall of Fame created a committee to select for annual induction players who had been at least 10-year veterans of the Negro Leagues and were ineligible for regular Hall election.

Sixteen

The Hot Box

We'll sort of ease you into this.

Ted Williams was almost as famous for the times he finished second in American League MVP voting as when he won in 1946 and 1949.

In 1941, he hit .406 and lost when Joe DiMaggio had his 56-game hitting streak and the New York Yankees won the pennant.

In 1942, Williams won the Triple Crown (leading the league in home runs, RBIs and batting average), but Joe Gordon of the Yankees won.

In 1947, after again having a Triple Crown he lost the closest MVP race in the history of Major League Baseball, coming short by a single point to the eventual winner, DiMaggio.

During one of those years, Williams had three teammates finish in the top 12 of the voting. Which season was it and who were they?

If you can get that correct there may be something wrong with you.

The answer is 1942. Johnny Pesky was third, Tex Hughson sixth and Bobby Doerr 11th.

When it comes to Red Sox trivia, these are some of the hardest of the hard, the ones that even the staunchest fans will struggle with and say: "Are you kidding me?"

The Hot Box

1. Which Boston Red Sox got into a game but due to an error his name didn't appear in the box score?
2. Who are the only players to suit up for the Red Sox from the following countries: Aruba, Denmark, Ireland, Jamaica, Netherlands, Poland, Scotland, Taiwan and Wales?
3. Through 2015 only 10 players in the American League, and 13 overall, had ever hit two grand slams in one game. Name the four who did it for the Red Sox and among them who hit them at home and who hit one from each side of the plate?
4. ... Now name the pitchers they hit them against.
5. Give the all-time Red Sox leaders at Fenway Park in batting average (minimum 2,000 at-bats), slugging percentage, hits, walks, stolen bases, doubles, triples, home runs, RBIs, wins, strikeouts, ERA (minimum 500 innings) and saves through 2014.
6. Name the all-time leaders for opposing players in those categories.
7. Name the 11 combinations of brothers who have played for the Red Sox.
8. Name the six father-son combinations, and the only grandfather-grandson tandem in Red Sox history.
9. List the military awards Ted Williams received during World War II and the Korean War.
10. Which four pitchers have hit grand slams for the Red Sox?
11. What four players have had a 10-RBI game for the Red Sox?
12. Which seven Red Sox pitchers have started an All-Star Game, and among them which two won the game's MVP award?
13. Name the seven players in American League history with 500 doubles, 450 home runs, 1,500 RBIs and 1,000 walks. (Hint: Four played for the Red Sox.)

14. Former Red Sox coach Al Bumbry was one of 54 Major League players who served in the military during the Vietnam War. Name them.

15. Who are the five Red Sox recipients of the Hutch Award, which is given annually to the Major League player who best exemplifies the character, fighting spirit and competitive desire of the late pitcher (Detroit 1939–53) and manager (Tigers, Cardinals, Reds), Fred Hutchinson?

16. The Red Sox have held spring training in 19 different cities. Name them.

17. Who are the three Red Sox players who have won the Tony Conigliaro Award for overcoming adversity?

18. Through 2014 the Red Sox had had eight players who were born in Japan. Name them. (Hint: One does not have a Japanese name.)

19. Name the five pitchers who have lost the most games for the Red Sox.

20. When Rick Renteria was selected in the first round of the 1980 June draft by the Pittsburgh Pirates at No. 20 overall, he began a stretch in which four of five draft selections went on to become Major League managers or general managers. Name the other three and the teams that made the selections.

21. What musician played Fenway Park during the 2004 season and vowed to break the curse?

22. What opposing pitcher hit an inside-the-park grand slam against the Red Sox at Yankee Stadium?

23. What opposing shortstop tied a Major League record with 28 fielding chances during a double-header against the Boston Red Sox?

24. Who are the six players who have hit a home run from both sides of the plate in a game for the Red Sox?

25. Who are the eight Red Sox who have hit pinch-hit grand slams?

26. Who are the eight Red Sox who have hit inside-the-park grand slams, and which player did it twice?

27. Who were the 10 players named to the Red Sox All-Time team as voted by fans in 1969?

Ted Williams receives the 1946 MVP Award from Joe Cashman, representing the Baseball Writers Association.

28. Who were the 11 players and manager named to the Red Sox All-Time team as voted by fans in 1982?

29. Who were the 11 players and manager who were second-team selections to the Red Sox All-Time team as voted by fans in 1982?

30. Dustin Pedroia needed just 1,048 games to hit his 300th double, the eighth fastest in Major League history. Name the seven batters that reached 300 doubles quicker.

31. The Red Sox have lost 23 players through five expansion drafts. Name them.

32. Who hit the most single-season home runs by position for the Red Sox through the 2014 season? (In other words most home runs by a catcher, first baseman …)

33. Who hit the most career home runs by position for the Red Sox (through 2014)?

34. Who are the 15 multiple winners of the Thomas A. Yawkey Award to the Red Sox Most Valuable Player?

35. The BoSox Club of Boston Man of the Year Award has been given out every year since 1967, when Rico Petrocelli was the first recipient, and has never had a repeat winner. Name the four coaches who have been honored.

Answers

1. On July 3, 1918, Harvey Fred "Red" Bluhm pinch-hit during a game, yet did not appear in the official box score. When the error was discovered his at-bat was added four decades later.

2. Aruba: Xander Bogaerts
Denmark: Olaf Henriksen
Ireland: Jimmy Walsh
Jamaica: Justin Masterson
Netherlands: Win Remmerswaal
Poland: Johnny Reder
Scotland: Bobby Thompson
Taiwan: Che-Hsuan Lin
Wales: Ted Lewis

3. Jim Tabor, July 4, 1939 vs. Philadelphia Athletics
Rudy York, July 28, 1946 vs. St. Louis Browns
Nomar Garciaparra, May 10, 1999 vs. Seattle Mariners
Bill Mueller, July 29, 2003, vs. Texas Rangers
Of the 13 players in Major League history who have hit two grand slams in one game Nomar Garciaparra's the only one do to it in his home stadium, and Bill Mueller's the only player in Major League history to do so from both sides of the plate.

4. George Castor and Lynn Nelson (Tabor), Tex Shirley (York), Brett Hinchliffe and Eric Weaver (Garciaparra); Aaron Fultz and Jay Poell (Mueller).

5. According to the Elias Sports Bureau:
Batting average: Wade Boggs .369
Slugging percentage: Ted Williams .652
Hits: Carl Yastrzemski 1,822
Walks: Ted Williams 1,031
Stolen bases: Jacoby Ellsbury 109
Doubles: Carl Yastrzemski 382
Triples: Harry Hooper 63
Home runs: Ted Williams 248
RBIs: Carl Yastrzemski 1,063
Wins: Tim Wakefield 98
Strikeouts: Roger Clemens 1,332
ERA: Carl Mays 1.80
Saves: Jonathan Papelbon 104

6. Again, according to Elias Sports Bureau:
Batting average: Fred McGriff .377
Slugging percentage: Frank Robinson .724
Hits: Al Kaline 218
Walks: Eddie Yost 126
Stolen bases: Rickey Henderson 47
Doubles: Al Kaline 49
Triples: Ty Cobb 17

Home runs: Mickey Mantle, Babe Ruth (tied) 38
RBIs: Lou Gehrig 152
Wins: Hooks Dauss 19
Strikeouts: Bob Feller 186
ERA: Lefty Grove 1.72
Saves: Mariano Rivera 36

7. Marty and Tommy Barrett, Cleo and Roy Carlyle, Billy and Tony Conigliaro, J.D. and Stephen Drew, Rick and Wes Ferrell, Alex and Milt Gaston, Johnnie and Joe Heving, Ed and Long Tom Hughes, Bob and Roy Johnson, Pedro and Ramon Martinez, Bob and Ed Sadowski.

8. Dolf and Doug Camilli, Ed Connolly, Sr. and Jr., Dick and Steve Ellsworth, Allen and Walt Ripley, Haywood and Marc Sullivan, and Joe and Smokey Joe Wood. John "Shano" Collins was an outfielder for the Red Sox in 1921–25, his grandson Bob Gallagher was a reserve player in 1972.

9. Naval Aviator Badge, Air Medal with two Gold Stars, Navy Unit Commendation, American Campaign Medal, Asiatic-Pacific Campaign Medal with Bronze Star, World War II Victory Medal, Navy Occupation Service Medal, National Defense Service Medal, Korean Service Medal with two Bronze Stars, United Nations Service Medal ROK Presidential Unit Citation.

10. Ellis Kinder, Wes Ferrell, Lefty Grove and Babe Ruth.

11. Nomar Garciaparra, Fred Lynn, Norm Zauchin and Rudy York.

12. Lefty Grove (1936), Mel Parnell (1949), Bill Monbouquette (1960), Dennis Eckersley (1982), Roger Clemens (1986), Pedro Martinez (1998), and Derek Lowe (2002). Clemens and Martinez both got the win and were named game MVP.

13. Lou Gehrig, David Ortiz, Rafael Palmeiro, Alex Rodriguez, Babe Ruth, Ted Williams and Carl Yastrzemski

14. Vic Albury, Matt Alexander, Frank Baker, Jim Bibby, Larry Biittner, Gene Brabender, Al Bumbry, Darrel Chaney, Bruce Christensen, Mike Davison, Ed Figueroa, Rich Folkers, Ted Ford, Larry French, Wayne Garrett, Roy Gleason, Chuck Goggin, Dave Goltz, Doug Griffin, Tom Heintzelman, Phil Hennigan, Jim Holt, Mike Jackson, Ray Jarvis, Bob Johnson, Bob Jones, Jerry Kenney, Jim Kern, Jerry Koosman, John Lowenstein, Garry Maddox, Jim Magnuson, Gene Martin, Larry Miller, George Mitterwald, Curt Motton, Thurman Munson, Bobby Murcer, Ray Newman, Scott Northey, Darrell Osteen, Harry Parker, Hal Quick, Dave Schneck, Mickey Scott, Rich Severson, Fred Stanley, Leroy Stanton, Earl Stephenson, Jim Strickland, Champ Summers, Jerry Terrell, Floyd Wicker, George Zeber. Source: Baseball Almanac.

15. Carl Yastrzemski (1967), Tony Conigliaro (1970), Andre Dawson (1994), Mark Loretta (2006) and Jon Lester (2008).

16. Charlottesville, Virginia, 1901
Augusta, Georgia, 1902
Macon, Georgia, 1903–06
Little Rock, Arkansas, 1907–08
Hot Springs, Arkansas, 1909–10; 1912–18
Redondo Beach, California, 1911
Tampa, Florida, 1919
Hot Springs, Arkansas, 1920–23

San Antonio, Texas, 1924

New Orleans, Louisiana, 1925–27

Bradenton, Florida, 1928–29

Pensacola, Florida, 1930–31

Savannah, Georgia, 1932

Sarasota, Florida, 1933–42; 1946–58

Medford, Massachusetts, 1943–44

Atlantic City, New Jersey, 1945

Scottsdale, Arizona, 1959–65

Winter Haven, Florida, 1966–93

Fort Myers, Florida, 1993–present

17. Bret Saberhagen (1998), Jon Lester (2007) and John Lackey (2013).

18. Tomo Ohka, Hideo Nomo, Dave Roberts, Daisuke Matsuzaka, Hideki Okajima, Takashi Saito, Junichi Tazawa, Koji Uehara.

19. Tim Wakefield (168), Cy Young (112), Roger Clemens (111), Bob Stanley and George Winter (both 97)

20. No. 22 Terry Francona by the Montreal Expos, Billy Beane by the New York Mets, and John Gibbons, also by the Mets. Francona was the Red Sox' manager from 2004–11.

21. Jimmy Buffett. Weeks later the Red Sox won the World Series.

22. New York Yankees ace Mel Stottlemyre during a 6–3 victory on July 20, 1965. He was the first pitcher in 55 years to hit an inside-the-park home run.

23. Ron Hanson of the Chicago White Sox.

24. Reggie Smith (who did it four times), Luis Alicea, Carl Everett, Bill Mueller, Jason Viratek and Victor Martinez. Mueller, of course, hit grand slams.

25. Mike Carp, Kevin Millar, Shea Hillenbrand, Rich Gedman, Rip Repulski, Charlie Maxwell, Clyde Vollmer and Vic Wertz (who as previously mentioned did it twice).

26. Mike Greenwell, Gary Geiger, Don Lenhardt, Jim Tabor, Shano Collins, Freddy Parent, Hobe Ferris and Jimmy Collins, while Duffy Lewis did it twice.

27. C Birdie Tebbetts

1B Jimmie Foxx

2B Bobby Doerr

3B Frank Malzone

SS Joe Cronin

OF Ted Williams

OF Carl Yastrzemski

OF Tris Speaker

RHP Cy Young

LHP Lefty Grove

Greatest player: Ted Williams

28. C Carlton Fisk

1B Jimmie Foxx

2B Bobby Doerr

3B Rico Petrocelli

SS Rick Burleson
OF Ted Williams
OF Carl Yastrzemski
OF Dwight Evans
RHP Cy Young
LHP Babe Ruth
RP Dick Radatz
Manager Dick Williams
Greatest player: Ted Williams
29. C Birdie Tebbetts
1B George Scott
2B Jerry Remy
3B Frank Malzone
SS Johnny Pesky
OF Jim Rice
OF Dom DiMaggio
OF Fred Lynn
RHP Luis Tiant
LHP Lefty Grove
PR Sparky Lyle
Manager Joe Cronin
30. Joe Medwick (916 games), Nap Lajoie (948), Hank Greenberg (988), Al Simmons (1,034), Todd Helton (1,041), and Nomar Garciaparra (1,047).
31. 1960 (8): To Los Angeles Angels: Jerry Casale, RHP; Jim Fregosi, INF; Fred Newman, RHP; Ed Sadowski, C; To Washington Senators: Jim Mahoney, INF; Tom Sturdivant, RHP; Haywood Sullivan, C; Willie Tasby, OF
1968 (6): To Kansas City Royals: Jerry Adair, INF; Joe Foy, INF; Dave Morehead, RHP; To Seattle Pilots: Dick Baney, RHP; Gary Bell, RHP; Darrell Brandon, RHP
1976 (5): To Seattle Mariners: Steve Burke, RHP; Luis Delgado, OF; Rick Jones, LHP; Dick Pole, RHP; To Toronto Blue Jays: Ernie Whitt, C
1992 (2): To Colorado Rockies: Jody Reed, INF; Eric Wedge, C
1997 (2): To Arizona Diamondbacks: Jeff Suppan, RHP; To Tampa Bay Devil Rays: Jim Mecir, RHP
32. Pitcher: 6 Wes Ferrell (1935), Earl Wilson (1965), Sonny Siebert (1971)
Catcher: 26 Carlton Fisk (1973, 1977)
First base: 50 Jimmie Foxx (1938)
Second base: 27 Bobby Doerr (1948, 1950)
Third base: 30 Butch Hobson (1977)
Shortstop: 40 Rico Petrocelli (1969)
Left field: 45 Manny Ramirez (2005)
Center field: 38 Fred Lynn (1979), Tony Armas (1984)
Right field: 36 Tony Conigliaro (1970)
Designated hitter: 47 David Ortiz (2006)

33. Pitcher: 17 Earl Wilson
    Catcher: 190 Jason Varitek
    First base: 217 Mo Vaughn
    Second base: 221 Bobby Doerr
    Third base: 131 Frank Malzone
    Shortstop: 177 Nomar Garciaparra
    Left field: 477 Ted Williams
    Center field: 123 Fred Lynn
    Right field: 315 Dwight Evans
    Designated hitter: 373 David Ortiz
34. Carl Yastrzemski (6), David Ortiz (5), Roger Clemens (4), Dwight Evans (4), Mo Vaughn (4), Ted Williams (4), Pedro Martinez (3), Rick Burleson (2), Carlton Fisk (2), Nomar Garciaparra (2), Jackie Jensen (2), Ellis Kinder (2), Frank Malzone (2), Dustin Pedroia (2) and Jim Rice (2).
35. Bill Fischer (1988), Wendell Kim (1997), Ron Jackson (2003), and Victor Rodriguez (2014).

About the Author

Christopher Walsh has been an award-winning sportswriter since 1990 and has authored 24 books. He's been twice nominated for a Pulitzer Prize, won three Football Writers Association of America awards, and received both the 2006 and 2014 Herby Kirby Memorial Award, the Alabama Sports Writers Association's highest honor for story of the year. Originally from Minnesota and a graduate of the University of New Hampshire, he currently works for Bleacher Report and resides in Tuscaloosa, Alabama.

His other books include:

Sweet 16: Alabama's Historic 2015 Championship Season, 2016

Cubs Triviology, 2016

Mets Triviology, 2016

Nick Saban vs. College Football, 2014.

100 Things Crimson Tide Fans Need to Know & Do Before They Die, 2008; updated 2012

Cowboys Triviology, 2011

Packers Triviology: 2011

Steelers Triviology: 2011

Huddle Up: New York Giants Football, 2009.

Huddle Up: Alabama Football, 2009.

Huddle Up: Michigan Football, 2009.

Huddle Up: Notre Dame Football, 2009.
Huddle Up: Ohio State Football, 2009.
Huddle Up: Oklahoma Football, 2009.
Huddle Up: Tennessee Football, 2009.
Huddle Up: Texas Football, 2009.
Who's No. 1? 100-Plus Years of Controversial Champions in College Football, 2007.
Where Football is King: A History of the SEC, 2006.
No Time Outs: What It's Really Like to be a Sportswriter Today, 2006.
Crimson Storm Surge: Alabama Football, Then and Now, 2005.
Return to Glory: The Story of Alabama's 2008 Season, 2009 (contributing writer).